Activating the Crew of
Spaceship Earth

A Guide Through Our Pivotal Planetary Transformation

John Schindler

ACTIVATING THE CREW OF
SPACESHIP EARTH

A GUIDE THROUGH OUR PIVOTAL PLANETARY TRANSFORMATION

Visionary author John Schindler's multifaceted journey has blended worldly expertise with metaphysical insight to be uniquely equipped to pen Activating the Crew of Spaceship Earth. He calls us into action as we stand at a pivotal juncture and must turn from the path where we plunder and waste the Earth's dwindling resources to our new path where we awaken our latent abilities and become true caregivers of our Planet Earth. We must steer humanity's trajectory toward a sustainable and harmonious future, or we face the dire consequences of our denial. We stand at the brink and together, we can choose renewal.

The book reveals that while modern society is faltering our consciousness is also awakening so we can meet the challenge. He spotlights how capitalism's commandeering of resources is a cancerous dynamic that conceals and exacerbates inequality, tribalism, and climate chaos that combine to threaten our very existence. In the book, John provides solutions and recommends clear ways to refocus from unhealthy psychology needing money accumulation towards unfolding our higher purpose.

The divisions we face as humans can dissipate, when new solutions emerge. By awakening our innate capacity, we will increase our empathy and act from our true heart. By blending ancestral wisdom, community building, economic reform, and technological innovation, he elucidates our opportunity for collectively awakening into a future with greater unity, expanded empathy and consciously directed purpose so we may embrace our sacred duty as planetary caregivers and write humanity's next chapter in balance with Earth's natural rhythms.

Designed, edited, and published by the Joyful Alchemists
TheJoyfulAlchemists.com | PO Box 719, Ojai, CA 93024

Copyright © 2023 by John Schindler

All rights reserved. No part of this book may be reproduced in any form or by any electronic or mechanical means, including information storage and retrieval systems, without permission in writing from the publisher, except by a reviewer, who may quote brief passages in a review.

ISBN 978-1-234567-91-3 (Ebook)

Table of Contents

Introduction 1

    The Book 11

    Our Home 14

    Our Path 19

I. Our Crossroads 25

    The Fourth Turning: Crisis and Renewal 30

        Trends that Increase the Crisis 32

        Dangers of Rapidly Advancing Technology 37

    The Urgency of a Paradigm Shift 41

        Recognizing the Gem of God 44

        Prophecies of Change 47

II. Turning Crisis into Opportunity 51

    Cyclical and Linear Time 53

    Learning from Cultural Wisdom 60

    Models for Creating Balance and Harmony 64

    Blue Zones Project 69

    Indigenous Wisdom 71

    Looking Forward into Culture 78

Seven Key Principles from the Star Trek Economic Model........79

III. The Village Model..88

    Fundamental Village Principles 89

    Modern Tribal Movements 92

    Cultivating Community Knowledge and Skills.........................95

    Envisioning the Future: From Consumption to Evolution 99

IV. Breaking Free of Unhealthy Restraints...................................103

    Diagnosing the Growing Problems with Capitalism 118

    Leadership By Unrestrained Greed or Guided Growth?............123

    Wealth Accumulation and the Widening Resources Gap.........125

    The Pink Elephant in the Room..136

V. The Cancer of Crony Capitalism: A Striking Analogy..............141

    Potential Reforms and Alternatives..146

    The Pursuit of Wealth Over Purpose.......................................156

    Treating the Cancer Within Us 161

VI. Embracing Spaceship Earth Ethics...163

    Redefining Wealth...165

    Embracing Minimalism...166

    From Consumption to Creative Expression............................168

    From Outer Conquering to Inner Nurturing..........................170

VII. The "We" Community is Key...173

    Community Integration 175

Valuing All Life 176
    Extraterrestrial Influence? 177
An Open Call to Participate 179
Where to Begin? 181
AI's Role in Managing Complexity 182
WayBeyond.ai - An Open Platform for Change 183
Bridging Grassroots and Government 185
A Glimpse Into Our Platforms 186
Managing Spaceship Earth: An Awakened Perspective 187

VIII. ABCs of Implementing Transformative Solutions 193
    A. Ecological Interventions: Healing the Earth 194
    B. Personal Strategies to Support the Collective Shift 203
    C. Economic Strategies for a Balanced Future 205
    D. Social Innovations: Building Communities of Change 207
    E. Intelligent Food Production 209
    F. Ecological Energy 213

IX. The Power & Role of Community 217
    ARC: A Blueprint for Future Communities 218
        Origins and Ethos of the ARC Model 219
        Key Features of the ARC Model 221
        ARC Model's Key Principles 223
    Transforming Struggle into Transformation 225

    The Axiom of Capability Meeting Challenges 228

    We Can Make This Happen.. 230

X. Rediscovering & Reintegrating Our Self............................... 237

    Recalling Our Latent Capabilities 244

    Another Theory of Relativity 247

    Reintegration of Our Greater Self................................ 252

    Activating Our Intuitive Abilities................................. 255

    What Do We Need to Shift? 263

    Uplifting Every Member... 264

    Uplifting Ourselves... 266

XI. Awakening Into Our Collective Destiny 269

    Envisioning a Healthy Earth for the Future 271

    Envisioning a Healthy Earth for the Future 272

    Embracing Our Proclivity to Evolve 274

    The Stars Start Here 276

XII. Anticipating Questions and Objections 278

Glossary of Terms.. 286

One step beyond everything is nothing
One step inside of nothing is everything
Patterns repeat from atoms to galaxies
Infinite possibilities within and without
Hear our shared destiny calling
Co-create our envisioned future
Spaceship Earth is our home

— John Schindler

Introduction

Our exquisite planet, Earth — seemingly the only planet we know of that supports complex life — navigates the cosmos with remarkable precision. It's now, however, facing significant instability due arguably to the choices and actions of its inhabitants. Many here have lost sight of true purpose and meaning, distracted by various indulgences and a global popular culture that often seems noisy and discordant.

In the midst of this, *she* (our celestial mothership) is striving to restore balance, giving us an opportunity to recognize a critical truth: **we need to shift from *indifference* to *active stewardship* to progress as a species.**

Yet, we find ourselves questioning: *What's the plan? Where is the leadership? Is there a clear direction to follow?*

We can no longer wait for the world to see the consequences of delaying action, which will affect not only us but also our children and future generations. This is the most significant reason for writing *this* book at *this* moment.

Along my path, I've encountered obstacles from powerful entities within the existing system in the past — as the pages unfold various moments of my story, you'll learn more about that. However, when I see a young activist like Greta Thunberg sacrificing her youth to confront world leaders about immediate climate action, it becomes clear that none of us have any excuse for silence or inaction.

We can't hide behind the all-too-compelling belief that the forces who maintain control over the status quo are too formidable. If one so young can show unwavering determination and courage to voice inconvenient truths and spark a global movement, then it's our duty to join her in this cause without further delay or excuses. The stakes are too high, the consequences too severe, for us to remain passive any longer. **The time for action is now.**

But who is John Schindler?

Why should my opinion matter on the subject of transforming the pending crisis we face? What kind of an expert am I? A scientist, a scholar, a political leader? I am *none* of these.

While I *am* an autodidact[1] — one who educates themselves — I am not a formally recognized academic authority. I'm an independent

---

1 https://en.wikipedia.org/wiki/Autodidacticism

thinker, a team leader, a generalist who can effectively coordinate specialists, and a guide in various industries and specialties. The intelligence within life itself has guided and prepared me from deep within to play a significant role in the collective endeavor required to address this convergence of Earth-shattering dynamics.

I wholeheartedly embrace what I see as **my duty** to support our society as we collectively navigate these critical environmental, economic, political, and social system challenges.

When you read this book and question whether the ideas and strategies within can genuinely make a tangible impact if implemented, my unequivocal response is a resounding "*yes!*" Should even a fraction of this plan be put into practice, the trajectory of human civilization would experience a substantial and unquestionable enhancement.

We must seek and implement these types of solutions to create a human order of life that is significantly less destructive due to the input and guidance of our activated crew of Spaceship Earth. In essence, I am here to convey that the universe has uniquely equipped me (and *many* like others) for the task at hand.

From a very early age, I was drawn towards the visual arts — feeling so gratified and accomplished when my paintings or sculptures were displayed in school. My father, being "realistic," used to tell me to put those dreams aside, get a real job, make a few million dollars, and, "... *then* you can do *all* the art you want." Otherwise, I would just live in poverty and be able to do nothing at all. If I countered his logic, my legitimate arguments were met with a brick wall of diminishment and a promise he would pull what little support he still provided in those early years of training in his "law of the jungle, eat or be eaten" philosophy of the world.

Heeding his seemingly well-meaning and *irrefusable* advice, I strategized how to rapidly accumulate wealth, with the ultimate goal of pursuing my *true* passion: **art**. I determined that the most efficient path to financial success lay in the realm of commercial real estate. At just 18 years old, I promptly passed my licensing exam. I dedicated myself to the capitalist ideal and sought affiliation with organizations like the Young Republicans, the Rotary Club, and other right-leaning groups, aspiring to gain access to influential networks.

My performance at the small yet notable real estate firm where I worked quickly earned me recognition as a local success story by the age of 19. Soon thereafter, I was approached and recruited by the world's largest commercial real estate company — now known as CBRE.

CBRE offered me to choose from one of 12 different cities in America, but I could not stay in San Diego because they wanted me out of that market where I was taking business from some of their agents. They set up a tour for me to interview at the various offices around the country where they had openings, which definitely impressed me. When I arrived in New Orleans and experienced the music, food, and social scene, I decided it was the perfect place for me and I moved there.

I was placed in the heavy industrial division, where I specialized in barge-draft and deep-water riverfront industrial properties. My clients predominantly came from sectors such as oil-field, tubular steel pipe, port and shipping, and the chemical corridor. I performed exceptionally well in my role as an industrial broker and swiftly rose to become one of the top producers in the region. I achieved significant financial success at a relatively young age. In 1983, at the age of 23, I made history in the office by closing a deal worth six figures — accomplished by transforming a Red Star yeast plant into an ethanol facility.

I used a portion of my share from the $350,000 fee to acquire a custom red 911 Porsche, which I imported, proudly affixing my personal "Red Star" license plate to this new symbol of my achievements. Against this performance-oriented backdrop, I found myself struggling to devote sufficient time to my art, and I grew increasingly aware of an inner void. In response, I made a conscious decision to contribute to a charitable endeavor known as The Workshop Way (WW), initiated by Sister Grace H. Pilon, a nun. She had devised an innovative "self-esteem-based education system" aimed at nurturing independent thinking and a passion for learning among students — a program that received acclaim from notable thinkers such as Jean Houston and Joseph Chilton Pearce for its significant educational value.

We commissioned a study through Tulane University that analyzed the data from Grace's early schools in Harlem, New York, which indicated her method could actually raise IQs and produce citizens who were more socially adept and stable, independent thinkers. The study further predicted that the underprivileged children in New Orleans who would go through the WW system from kindergarten through 12th grade might actually meet or exceed the average entrance exam score of those accepted into Harvard. The WW needed $6 million to open three experimental pilot schools in the most troubled areas of New Orleans.

With deep faith in the importance of this program, I approached a multi-billionaire client of mine, who had purchased an investment property from me a year or so before. He had soon afterward developed a mentor-like relationship with me, taking me under his wing. I respected and looked up to this gentleman, who in addition to being incredibly successful, also displayed personal qualities I truly admired. He was very receptive to the WW pilot schools and agreed to give them the entire $6 Million. As a formality, he had to first run it past the Republican party, who he had to let conduct a "sniff" test before he contributed money to any charitable organizations.

A month later he came to town and we met for lunch. He told me that when he ran it up the ranks, he was informed in response that they did not want an infestation of free-thinking and academically superior minority applicants getting into Harvard. They threatened that if he gave even one dollar to this organization, they would pull all support from him and disassemble his empire.

He was shaken — but not as much as I was *shocked*. This man was my role model and represented a level of personal achievement and freedom I was striving for. It was a real eye-opener that even *he* was still on a leash.

Soon I was advised by my manager that I should drop this particular charitable work, because it was alienating some of my clients. I also received a call from a client in NY to whom I had sold the Red Star Yeast Plant for conversion into an ethanol plant, which was a clean industry. He informed me that they were being leveraged by the port of New Orleans to pay exorbitant fees to use their own dock. They refused to pay what he called "extortion" and informed me they would shut down the plant. Other projects and assignments also started to unravel. Another executive from a prominent company who was considering building a factory in a large industrial park backed out and then told me I should consider the consequences of "luring companies into that pack of wolves in Louisiana."

While these setbacks were somewhat disconcerting, I was now 25 years old and living what many would consider "the good life." I received invitations to all the right events, had influential friends, and even found myself listed in two publications as one of the most eligible bachelors in New Orleans and the South. My income had soared to the top 1% of men in America, a level that, for most, seemed unattainable.

And... it's important to note that extreme wealth doesn't always equate to high personal income. The 1% personal income I achieved was far from the wealth level of the top 1% in terms of net worth in America. Many among this group have no conventional jobs, don't generate ordinary income, and consequently, pay little to no taxes.

My work was very high-stress, but I countered it with rigorous physical exercise, training more than fifteen hours a week for Ironman triathlons. I was in super shape, but then one day, I just passed out while at work. After extensive tests, I was diagnosed with heavy metal poisoning, contaminated with the same heavy metals that the companies I represented used in the oilfield plants I frequented. I was aware that some of these companies and plants were coming under attack by a new generation of protestors against pollution. The plant managers I knew assured me that their complaints were entirely unfounded. Was my karma coming back onto me for supporting extreme polluters? I was unsure what the truth was and started looking deeper and certain patterns began to emerge that created increasing doubt and uncertainty.

Once I began to open my eyes to information that was opposed to my own self-interest, my confidence cracked, and my previous view of my perfect world model started to crumble. In the spring of 1986 at the company awards banquet, where I was to receive a high honor, because my commissions were projected to exceed seven figures that year, I recognized I was becoming a high lieutenant for industrialists exploiting the earth for profits. I found it increasingly difficult to work for them and resigned. I believe I had a *spiritual metanoia*, which is a change of mind brought about in repentance. My company defined it as a mental and emotional breakdown.

Joseph Campbell, the renowned mythologist and writer, often spoke about the idea of climbing the ladder only to realize it was leaning against the wrong wall as a metaphor for the pursuit of goals and dreams that may not align with one's true passions and values. This concept was central to his work on the *hero's journey* and the idea of finding one's *bliss*. Campbell emphasized the importance of introspection and self-discovery to ensure that the path one is on leads to a fulfilling and meaningful life, rather than one that is driven solely by external expectations or societal pressures. This was my *exact* predicament.

After I stepped out of my company, my mentor client billionaire offered me a very lucrative role in his firm. When I turned it down, he was concerned for my future and sadly exclaimed that I was choosing a very hard road. He explained that he agreed in principle with my ideals, but life is full of many problems and challenges, and 95% of the challenges can be fixed with more money. Although I saw the validity in his pragmatic view, I found this perspective tragic, rather than inspiring. In hindsight, maybe I could have done more good by staying in the club and trying to help my wealthy clients deploy their formidable resources in more conscientious ways? Instead, I viewed them as a destructive club and chose to strike out in a new direction.

My transition was neither smooth nor painless. I lost many relationships, respect, and influence along with my increasing high income. One of my main personal realizations was that I had been living in a bubble of my own projections, seeing the extension of my own ego and desires as reality. In my movie, other people were secondary players to my leading role. I was so caught up in the grandeur of my own existence that I did not realize how much I was missing all around me. One of the main aspects of life I had overlooked was the degree of struggle that so many people were suffering with in New Orleans just to survive and make ends meet.

Previously, I believed the system was functioning perfectly fairly. And it *had* been… for me.

While my financial coffers no longer overflowed, my life became full of rich experiences and wonder. While it took time to realize, the Universe was now teaching me "to accomplish almost anything, with next to nothing, at any given moment." I believe that I have been put onto a path to pioneer new models and methods of value creation, engaging forms of energy other than capital. It took me a while still to realize that these ways of creating had been done for most of human history. And while it has been the dominant force during my lifetime, this reign of capital has only been relatively recent in human history as the driving force it is now.

One of my recent realizations has been around community and creative vision. I recognize how understanding the problems is only the very beginning of the equation. The power is in creating the solutions; and learning to live life like an enlightened human being would need to in order to have human civilization flourish in 500,000 years from now. I want to be one of those pioneers that helps model and establish that lifestyle. Further, by focusing our powerful transcendental gifts that we possess inside, we, as the center of our own inner-dimensional existence, can Co-Create a more Heavenly state of existence here, now, on earth even if we, as the collective, are going through difficult challenges and the corresponding changes.

While money is now clearly a "god-like power," I believe that in coping with these massive challenges, we are guided to create with divine intelligence, which may even challenge the throne of capitalism.

I believe in the mystic powers as described in Hebrews 11:1 "Now faith is the substance of things hoped for, the evidence of things not seen." I interpret this scripture to mean that when sincere humans align their intention in faith, the alignment itself is a form of evidence that the goal is likely to manifest. I am fully committed to our collective activation so we can evolve our social system and preserve the Earth's ecosystem.

Please, align with me, and let's make this transformation happen!

The Book

Activating The Crew of Spaceship Earth is an invitation to expand our understanding of our capacity to evolve and embark on this transformational and spiritual journey. This book challenges all belief systems. It is intended to expand all belief systems. For those rare *enlightened beings*, I believe that enlightenment is a collective experience that results when our shared vibration rate resonates us all into a higher frequency. So, while there may be some that are more aware than some others, everyone is either enlightened or no one is fully enlightened.

It is more apparent than ever to me that life will no longer allow us to avoid addressing the issues explored herein. As a leading academic authority, Jem Bendell portends in his book, **Breaking Together**, that our collective over-consumption of resources, and deficit spending is rapidly breaking down our system. This structure, based upon never-ending growth and heavily top-loaded economic wealth, has set the stage for an ecological, economic, and social collapse. Based on the math, the events simmering, dwindling resources, and the ecological imbalance, equate to the free-market system being very likely to come apart soon. I ask you — in favor of what alternative?

As a parent of two teenagers and in consideration of the well-being of all future generations, I earnestly implore those who can hear and see to unite with each other in mutual goodwill. Together, let's forge a path away from what appears to be an impending catastrophe if we fail to seek alternatives to these deteriorating political and economic systems.

Today our champions take unorthodox forms. Greta Thunberg calls out to the world decrying how our climate and ecological emergency is "the biggest crisis humanity has ever faced." While she may have given up on presidents and prime ministers, kings and queens, politicians and leaders — their excuses, empty words, and inactions — she has not given up on humanity. "It's up to you and me," she says. "No one else will do it for us."

I am not a doomsday thinker, but it is evident to me that if we do not make the obvious and clearly needed shifts in our behavior right away, continued breakdown is inevitable and will affect a level of general existential pain that few in the modern world can fathom.

Nevertheless, I believe this imminent crisis could serve as the catalyst necessary to mobilize us and instigate the changes needed before the escalating hardships become insurmountable. If we tap into our intrinsic, albeit dormant, capacities, we have the potential to surpass the constraints of our societal challenges and, out of necessity, evolve into more enlightened individuals. My objective is to communicate how we can collectively navigate these waters, which necessitate collaborative solutions, and to do so promptly - as in, right *now!*

This book examines the dominant economic, ecological, and social problems through varied lenses. By pinpointing challenges, focusing capabilities, and proposing solutions, I hope to catalyze a paradigm shift that expands the reader's confidence to understand how we can collectively adjust and realign our habits and systems to facilitate this ***pivotal planetary transformation.*** Spaceship Earth bangs ever more loudly on our doors, begging us to come out of our air-conditioned boxes and tend to the garden.

In discussing various topics, I present ideas concisely within a compact framework, which requires a fast-paced and occasionally unexpected writing style. This diverse approach is deliberate, designed to shift your perspective away from conventional norms and reveal less obvious connections. By examining the intersections of scientific trends, cultural philosophies, spirituality, and economic and political policies in this manner, you may discover the significance and purpose of your unique blend of skills and passions. This newfound awareness can inspire meaningful action as we work together as crew members aboard Spaceship Earth.

I've made deliberate choices that may seem to leave certain areas less developed. This is intentional and part of my strategy. I excel at coordinating specialists from various fields for a single project. The details will be explored in future works, with input from the crew of

Spaceship Earth to solve logistical problems. In this book, I aim to help you see the intricate connections among these elements and how they form a cohesive whole. Not everyone is comfortable with this level of detail, much like a conductor orchestrating a diverse ensemble to create a symphony.

Adjust your viewpoint and, with any luck, the broader panorama will manifest itself, much akin to a "MagicEye" picture - a meticulously designed visual puzzle that hinges on grids and precision for its desired outcome: Cross your eyes. Well, perhaps squint instead. Attempt to ease into the view… *Hey!*… and just like that, the image materializes. Every illusion is decipherable, provided you know the way to observe it.

Our Home

Some people strive to lead the way and make the critical shifts we must to survive, but the majority of us are simply trying to live our lives and enjoy the time we have left. We try to be good people, but we see these problems as just too big and beyond our control. Can we afford to be passive passengers on this voyage when we know our affairs are not being properly managed? When will we be willing to step forward and act on what we know is right? Can we really be that oblivious to the interconnected fates of all of us aboard?

The time to awaken and shift is right now. We still have an opportunity to adjust our direction and we must embrace our collective roles as caretakers on this cosmic vessel. It is our privilege to support her inhabitants with courage and joy. If we do not step forward with clear intention, then this crossroads will demand our monumental awakening through drastic means. It is time for us to recognize our shared responsibility, to guide Spaceship Earth, to create a new phase of balance and renewal. But how can we traverse this growing challenge?

I do not suggest we should "fix" the world. I do not use such language because **there is nothing wrong with the world**. It is an amazing Omni-University of higher learning for our souls and a diverse, magnificent habitat for the myriad forms of life that inhabit her. The problem in the world is how we function as a society, as *almost-humane beings*. We do not need to change the world or our fundamental nature to fix the problems. In its most basic sense, we need to simply recognize how certain systems that once served us as a species have now become out of synch with our very tangible and urgent needs as a society, and must be adjusted. The problem is in the system and structure, *not* the people (per se), *not* the world.

We are remarkable beings, a blend of awareness, intelligence, and sensitivity, connected to our divine source in a physical, living form. To make this transition, we must acknowledge our true nature. No need to change or be more than we are; we are enough. When we see our shared intention to responsibly care for our world and grasp the issues clearly, we can navigate this societal transformation with grace and swiftness. Perhaps this is our primary purpose in being here and now.

To open new territory in our perspective, I will shift among the following core thematic principles:

Integrating Ancient Wisdom

To correct our trajectory, we will glean insight from the ancients. Indigenous cultures, aligned with nature's rhythms, contain profound wisdom passed down through generations. Their reverence for the land and spirit of mutual aid has allowed communities to thrive sustainably since time immemorial.

We will distill timeless principles from varied sources — diverse native traditions, mystical schools of thought, and epochal spiritual philosophies, which hold seeds of truth relevant to the present hour. But insight alone is insufficient. To translate wisdom into collective renewal, we must mesh it with innovation.

Look into Futuristic Models

The synthesis of ancient knowledge with futuristic cultural expressions and cutting-edge science will amalgamate into a foundation for the systemic changes required. By bridging these realms and using the best of the past and future, we can co-create a vision that honors our heritage and grounds us in the ways of nature with a tech-integrated future.

Championing Community and Collectivism

In modern times, with knowledge democratized, power concentrated, and lives increasingly virtual, the social fabric now frays. For eons, however, shared purpose and unity bound clans and villages into cohesive wholes — members contributing, supporting and celebrating each other's journey through life.

These communal roots must be unearthed and revitalized if we are to find balance. Competition and isolation must yield to cooperation and interdependence. Lives of meaning must arise through mutual upliftment. Hardships must be faced communally, joys shared abundantly.

This reawakening of collective spirit can permeate all facets of society — from governance to economics. Participative models, where each voice holds equity, offer insights into the design of people-centric systems. Such an ethos of shared responsibility provides an antidote to the disenfranchisement and fragmentation plaguing our age.

Healing Humanity's Relationship with Nature

Flourishing civilizations in the past lived as an integral part of the natural world, not dominators set apart. Their prosperity flowed from the respectful partnership with the land, air and water. When resources were overly exploited, the communities suffered directly and it was clear adjustments had to be made. There was no massive redistribution machine to conceal the problems behind a global supply chain or a masterful spin campaign to conceal the inevitable.

To recognize the truth and right our course, humanity must rekindle this harmonic bond with nature ruptured by industrialization and greed. The path starts by observing patterns in the biological world and seeking to align our innovations with life's wisdom. It continues by adopting regenerative practices that actively heal and nurture Earth's ecosystems.

At its essence, it requires us to profoundly realize that our destiny is entwined with the collective — all people, creatures, and life forces are interdependent. By acting from this heartfelt truth, we can restore humanity's friendship with nature. And Earth, once and always magnanimous, will share her bounty so that all species may thrive in harmonious balance.

Transforming Capitalism

Unrestrained capitalism has steered humanity towards believing in "consumer economics" — a form of temporary insanity that blends material excess with spiritual poverty and calls it *progress*. The concentration of wealth is ever-shifting to favor fewer beings with uncalloused hands with heavily calloused spirits — while multitudes starve. These fortunes were accumulated by claiming ownership to and ravaging Earth's resources and living systems; while this progress is measured and concealed behind pushing for endless economic growth that no longer can be sustained. Stories are constantly spun by the bought and paid-for media to support the myths of unbridled capitalism and invalidate ecological concerns, even as entire ecosystems crumble and hundreds of species vanish every day.

These perils demand courageous reckoning. However, discarding capitalism wholly may yield equal or worse outcomes. Money as an exchange of resources is healthy, needed, and valuable for a global society to flourish. However, turning over the reins of our planetary destiny to self-serving exploiters in the name of a free-market economy is simply suicidal insanity. The task ahead is not destruction but wise reform — redirecting capitalism's immense energies into socially equitable and ecologically regenerative outcomes.

This transformation requires moral imagination on a scale hitherto unseen. Regulation, innovation, and collective action must synergize to redesign global markets in service of shared prosperity so that economic exchange enhances lives while replenishing the biological source of our common home.

All of these principles will combine and aid us as we **_awaken into our collective destiny_**. The transformation required spans all dimensions — political, economic, social, and spiritual. But it begins within, in the human heart yearning for purpose and connection. As each person rediscovers their intrinsic wholeness, society too will grow healthier.

The journey ahead will not be easy. But guided by wisdom, ancient and modern, we can create a future of equity, a sustainable and vibrant community. The stars themselves are not even the limit of our potential — for when souls awaken to their divine nature, the impossible becomes merely the next horizon to bring vision into the realm of the possible.

Our Path

There is a well-known saying that "the world will never change until people do." On some levels, this is evidently true. On the other hand, as Margaret Mead so clearly stated, "Never doubt that a small group of thoughtful, committed citizens can change the world; indeed, it's the only thing that ever has."

One of my mentors and friends is a change management expert and author, Daryl Conner. He once shared with me the concept that in change management, "People only change when the pain of not changing outweighs the discomfort of changing." It seems we have a considerable amount of motivation heading our way in the form of challenges and difficulties. Perhaps this is the nudge we need to break free from the inertia of avoidance and embrace transformation.

The term "human" is derived from the Latin word *humus*, which means earth or ground. I initially hoped it was linked to "humane" — signifying an attitude of placing the needs of other living beings on par with our own. However, "human" traces back to the Latin term *humanus*, a combination of *homo* meaning man, and *humus* meaning earth. This suggests that humans are creatures of the earth, intimately connected to the natural world. Although "human" didn't originate from "humane," the word *humanus* also conveyed "having the qualities of compassion or benevolence typically associated with human beings."

Modern life may cloud this connection, but traces of it persist within us. Our compassion, our desire to nurture life, our appreciation of beauty — these qualities indicate our belonging to something larger. We're not passive travelers on Spaceship Earth; we're active participants on a cosmic journey. By gazing at the stars, we acknowledge that our presence here isn't random. We're not mere biological forms that happened to evolve on a planet; rather, we are extensions of a greater source, expressions of creation beyond our complete understanding, yet well within our capacity for participation.

If we aren't accidental, what is the foundational idea of our existence? This sparks other questions: Where are we heading? Does this journey have a specific destination? Is it a physical place or a desired outcome? Do we possess a genuine purpose? Is it devastation, utopia, evolution, or extinction? If there's something more for us, what is it? I'm compelled to share the answers I've uncovered, as are many others. My hope is that this book might help you unearth insights from within your own consciousness, not passively, but through your future choices and resulting actions, contributing to our *collective awakening*.

As we move through the 21st century, our power to shape landscapes and wield nuclear weapons confronts us with an existential dilemma. It's akin to children playing with explosives, captivated by the bright light and loud noises but not fully comprehending the potential destruction they could unleash. This precarious position bestows upon us a profound responsibility, whether we acknowledge it willingly or not. When we possess the capability to endanger all life on Spaceship Earth, it becomes our duty to ensure its preservation.

Are you ready to embrace your role? To shift from a passive **passenger** to an active and caring **crew member**? Ready or not, we're on this journey together. Hand in hand, heart to heart, we'll build a future in harmony with Earth and the natural order of things, allowing us to then reach for the stars.

ACTIVATING THE CREW OF SPACESHIP EARTH

First, we must care for our home, and then the myriad possibilities will unfold and reveal themselves. This is our shared path — change is not imposed by chance or fate but driven by conscious choices, guided by courage, care, and wisdom. We walk as shepherds, not masters, cherishing Earth instead of conquering it. In turn, life will cherish us and unveil its deeper, hidden secrets.

Part 1
The Wake Up Call

The world remains the closest it has ever been to the symbolic hour of the apocalypse, with the Doomsday Clock set once again to 90 seconds to "midnight" for 2024. The Doomsday Clock is a metaphorical representation of how close humanity is to destroying the world via nuclear weapons, climate change and other means.

I.
our crossroads

Throughout history, many moments have arisen that tested the mettle of civilizations, challenging humanity to face turning points. These "crossroads," demand reflection, adaptation, and growth for its inhabitants to emerge in a positive direction. Today, we stand at such a profound global crossroads that it will impact all life on Earth going forth into the future. One way or another our destiny will be cast over the next few decades.

After I left commercial real estate, my financial world crumbled, and I found myself at a crossroads, lost and needing to find a completely different life path. A project I had previously invested in heavily melted down, wiping out my savings. A cabin in the woods that I moved into in Tuscaloosa, Alabama got struck by lightning and destroyed my tax records. I ignorantly called the IRS to ask what I should do and they told me that I should not have called them because now they would have to tax me on my gross income knowing I could not prove my write-offs. Instantly, what would have been a $75,000 refund turned into a $150,000 tax debt. I was sinking and I needed to make a couple hundred bucks just to get gas money to drive to a friend's cabin in the Ozarks, where I planned to live off the land and lick my wounds for a while until I figured out my next steps.

I convinced my friend to hire me to build shelves in his production truck that he had rented to hold camera equipment for the first high-definition TV movie, *The Jazz Man*. When I arrived, they were fighting over a major problem. My friend was supposed to have a generator mount made for the front of his truck to hold a special generator for the computers, but he could not get it done for the $6,000 budgeted. The shoot was to start the following morning and they could not run the million-dollar camera computers without the mounts for the generator which provided the clean power. It would cost the production over $250,000 for each day of delay.

While they argued over who would pay for this fiasco, I went outside, dropped the bumper, traced the mounts, and went to a steel shipyard down the road where I found an older welder/fabricator to help. Two hours later, I returned and they were still arguing. I grabbed Barry Rebo, the producer from NY, dragged him outside, and to his surprise, I had fixed the problem. I charged him only $800, not the $6,000 budgeted, but that was still $400 more than I paid the welder. I had my Ozark departure money and a bit extra for some canned food.

But instead of working just that day, I was hired for the entire shoot at a much higher rate, despite having no training, education, or experience in filmmaking. They thought I was a genius. I had solved their problem and that was enough to get me into a position they invented, the "Utility Man" to the camera department. My old world had crumbled, but I somehow had stumbled onto a new path. Or did the Universe reset my direction to what it should be?

Two years later in 1988, I directed an environmental documentary, *Eco-Mardi Gras — Ecology is a Personal Statement* which targeted a $2 billion plant slated for Louisiana's Chemical Corridor. They were labeled as one of the world's worst polluters and had been kicked out of Korea. The new plant was estimated to pump over 22 tons of toxic chemicals a month into the Mississippi River that would enter the New Orleans drinking water supply. Due to the protests we staged for the production, they canceled the project. This was a demonstration in no uncertain terms that I was now on the "other side."

We are now at a critical crossroads and need to shift our collective life paths. Through our short-sighted planning and almost unfathomable resource depletion over the past century, and the overall environmental degradation, we have ensured future generations will inherit a world substantially depleted of resources, with significantly diminished and damaged ecosystems and a harsh and volatile climate. The validity of this claim may still be plausibly denied by the hierarchy hellbent on spinning deception while they exploit every drop they can, but the physics of the imbalance, depletion, and poisoning of our Earth's systems that sustain us are very quantifiable through scientific observation for anyone who wants to see the truth.

When I was a young boy, my father managed a large sales force for a major life insurance company. He hired some of the top trainers to hold seminars for his men, and he allowed me to attend. One of those trainers was a profound man, the American author, salesman, and motivational speaker named Zig Ziglar. I very much respected and adored him. As a child, Zig would recognize me as I ran ahead of my father to find him when we picked him up in the airport. He was an early mentor, and one of the main principles that he taught me was that there are huge advantages in addressing challenges that we face at the earliest possible moment rather than putting them off until the last minute.

The advantages of taking on challenges early rather than putting them off are many and significant. Among those advantages are:

- Life tends to increase pressure on us to make needed changes by turning up the heat.
- By handling needed changes early, we thereby minimize the pain and discomfort that they cause if they are not handled on a timely basis.
- The cost and penalties of not making needed changes or handling our responsibilities on a timely basis just go up and up, like not paying a parking ticket on time.
- We make better decisions when we have less pressure on us because we think more clearly in a peaceful state of mind and are more composed.
- We often have more resources to work with to make the changes because we have not depleted our reserves as much.
- We have more peace of mind after it's been accomplished because we no longer have that task weighing on our minds and burning up our schedules.

- We naturally emerge as Leaders because we are among the first to accomplish the task and therefore can help others do it more easily.
- It leads us to become more visionary because instead of our focus being pulled into the past, we are free to address the future in an uncluttered fashion.

These principles have proven beneficial in my life, assisting me in adapting swiftly and managing transitions effectively. I've often found that I complete tasks promptly in both professional and personal settings, affording me the capacity to undertake additional projects or assist others with theirs. I hold a strong aversion to procrastination and have observed its negative impact on those who engage in it.

Now more than ever, I see procrastination working against us individually and collectively as a species and society as the challenges we face grow in magnitude and the threat becomes more critical and dangerous by the day.

Are the conditioned patterns, obstacles, and forces that impede our recognition of the need for change formidable? *Absolutely*. But are these obstacles and forces more perilous than the potential catastrophic consequences of inaction? **Absolutely not.**

The ecological threats we face are enormous, and the need for swift solutions is urgent. Therefore, I firmly believe we have a profound responsibility to actively harness our collective intelligence and abilities for this transformation. Ignoring or postponing these changes only exacerbates the imminent perils, putting both present and future generations at risk. This is not an exaggeration; scientific evidence and forecasts clearly highlight the risks.

While emotions understandably run high given the high stakes, it's crucial to take level-headed yet decisive action. It's time for introspection, deep reflection on our shared responsibilities, and a rapid mobilization of resources to transition to a sustainable paradigm. Lives are at stake, and we have viable solutions within reach. We can't afford further delay or complacency. The future calls for us to awaken, unite, and act resolutely to safeguard the well-being of all on this fragile planet we call home.

The Fourth Turning: Crisis and Renewal

Based on the significant and paradigm-altering research conducted by Neil Howe and William Strauss regarding "The Fourth Turning" (in their book by the same name) — which is also referred to as the "Turning of Crisis" — and Howe's 2023 publication, *The Fourth Turning is Here*, we are currently at a critical juncture in American history.

Their model is derived from deep research and analysis of centuries of patterns and cycles. It groups these cycles into discernible patterns called *saeculum*, spanning roughly 80 to 100 years, roughly the length of the longest human lifespans of the period. Each saeculum encompasses four distinct "Turnings" — High, Awakening, Unraveling, and Crisis. According to Howe and Strauss, we currently find ourselves navigating the treacherous waters of the Crisis, a period of profound upheaval and monumental change.

This current saeculum commenced around the Great Depression following World War II, placing us firmly within the Crisis stage, slated to culminate in the mid-2030s. As with prior Crises, this period forms a pivotal bridge from a "destructive phase" marked by division and disintegration, towards a following "constructive phase" that harbors the promise of rebuilding and renewal. It is therefore very likely that the full magnitude of our various cultural, ecologic, economic, and political crises will come to some form of a climax and then resolution by the mid-2030s.

Transitions of such magnitude are seldom without turmoil and this turning of crisis looks to be building into a metaphorical "perfect storm" of danger and magnitude and may culminate with a major upheaval unparalleled in recent human history. The destructive phase compels us to dismantle obsolete systems and structures that no longer serve our society's needs. The constructive phase, though symbolizing hope and rebirth, requires significant disruption to be birthed.

We have the formidable responsibility of dismantling the old to pave the path for the rise of new and innovative paradigms. This process is both demanding and crucial. The Crisis Turning we find ourselves in is made even more intense by the tumultuous challenges and unprecedented dilemmas before us. These factors heighten the risk of this crisis period and provide stark reminders of the strained relationship we hold with Earth, our home *and* our life-sustaining ecosystem.

The Crisis Turning looms as a dark cloud on our collective horizon, portending significant hardship and painful shifts. Yet, within this seemingly grim narrative, there resides hope. The very intensity of the immense wealth disparity, social and political polarization, and our growing ecological crises might serve as the catalyst for significant collective action, for making radical changes of certain long-standing institutions and revising financial models that have held the problematic systems firmly in place.

As we navigate the Turning of Crisis, we must seize the opportunities it presents. Despite the enormity of the challenges and the difficulties along the path, the potential for transformation is unparalleled. We are presented with an opportunity to redefine our societal and financial structures, to adjust our course, to repair our strained relationship with Earth, and to provide the loving maintenance she needs. Now is the time for us to reshape our communities, realign our societies, and reimagine our future in harmony with each other and with Earth. The Turning of Crisis is more than a period of change, it is a call to action. As the inhabitants and the crew of Spaceship Earth, we must heed this call for the survival and flourishing of all life.

Trends that Increase the Crisis

The pace at which we have squandered Earth's bounty and accumulated toxic waste in mere decades will surely be seen by future generations as an era of ignorance and myopia. A primary motivation for this book is that **I hear the pleas of our suffering descendants from the future**, asking us to change course and preserve some form of resources for them. They remind me that they are us, our offshoots, a continuation of our tree of life.

Over the last century, we've depleted energy reserves formed over a billion years. The sustainability of such consumption raises critical questions about our responsibility to future generations. Is the marginal progress worth squandering the vast majority of tangible energy sources? The notion of "DEVO," the De-Evolution of Man, as suggested by the band, prompts reflection on whether our trajectory truly signifies advancement. Would individuals alter their behavior if confronted with the prospect of being reborn as our descendants, inheriting a world ravaged by our reckless consumption?

Some people talk like we may have the option in the future to move out into space and develop other worlds. While that is not completely beyond any future possibility, I would point out that the best building material for future generations to create spacecraft and space stations would be manufactured from petroleum products. Over the last 75 years, we have literally burnt up the majority of the world's fuel reserves for space development, and why? To create combustion in primitive motors, to scurry about in confusion with no meaningful direction, while poisoning the environment and accumulating massive trash reserves? The underutilization of the world's petroleum reserves is simply a reflection of our overall short-sightedness and miscalculations in planning a future that can be sustained. Our deficit living, such as consuming the majority of the world's energy reserves in less than a century, may not yet be recognized by some as the disaster it is for the future, but if we manage to move forward intact, it certainly will be.

Energy and sustainability expert Nate Hagens has discussed the concept of what he calls "the great simplification" in the context of resource constraints and the future of society. Hagens argues that our current way of life, which is heavily dependent on fossil fuels and finite resources, is unsustainable in the long term. He suggests that the Earth's fuel reserves are finite, and the depletion of these reserves will lead to a significant simplification or downsizing of our complex and energy-intensive lifestyles.

Hagens emphasizes that as we deplete non-renewable resources, such as fossil fuels, we will need to transition to more sustainable and simpler ways of living. This transition could involve reducing energy consumption, rethinking our economic systems, and finding alternative sources of energy. The "great simplification" refers to the idea that we will need to adapt to a world with fewer available resources and a more modest way of life.

We must swiftly curb our mismanagement of resources and ecological systems, and change course towards responsible planetary stewardship before it's too late. Only by ensuring the sustainability of Earth can we preserve the potential to one day fuel the technological advances and societal maturity required to venture responsibly beyond our atmosphere.

However, if we continue pillaging terrestrial resources blindly, depleting the very materials and neglecting the very life support systems essential for spacefaring capabilities, we will have foreclosed any feasible future among the stars.

Our window to master living sustainably on this Earth is rapidly closing. This must be our paramount concern; the health of our planetary home is the essential prerequisite for any ambitious interstellar dreams.

Our current landscape is marred by multifarious challenges and examples of our planetary mismanagement, each amplifying the other.

- Climate Change
- Biodiversity Decline
- Modern Food Supply Production Problems
- Ocean System Depletion from Over-Fishing
- Resistant Superbugs and Diseases
- Societal Disparities
- Widening Economic Gaps
- Energy Demands and Shortages
- Nuclear Power Waste Buildup
- Diminishing Resources Competition
- Supply Chain Logistical Breakdowns
- Misguided Leadership for Special Interest Groups
- Military Buildup and Weapons of Mass Destruction
- Despair and Uncertainty In Our Youth
- Mental Health and Drug Dependency Issues

Certainly, this list of crisis issues might seem overwhelming, yet, inside of this massive collection of problems, there is also unparalleled opportunity for us to emerge with levels of collective mastery heretofore unimagined.

Could it be that the scale of the challenges we face is a reflection of the immense pressure needed to inspire us to overcome complacency and unlock the incredible potential within us? There's a saying that suggests the greater our capabilities, the higher the summits we must ascend. In order to counterbalance the unconscious depletion of our world's resources and mend the wounds inflicted upon it, we must step forward as planetary caregivers, armed with exceptional skills and a conscientious commitment to nurture life and one another back to health.

This transformation seems like a purpose worth pursuing, a goal that gives life real meaning. I am fully committed to this cause. Are you?

It's evident that our understanding of this era and the path we choose as a species and civilization will undeniably shape our collective trajectory. It will determine whether we steer ourselves towards a precipice, descending into a prolonged period of decline and suffering, or if we raise our awareness and actions to unveil a path toward unparalleled societal progress.

In the chapters to follow, we will seek to understand more deeply the nature of our challenges and dig for the glimmering gems of opportunity that hide within them.

Dangers of Rapidly Advancing Technology

Technology can work with us or against us depending on how it is applied. By using scientific breakthroughs judiciously, we can support our highest aspirations. However, we have also developed technologies that escalate the devastation of Earth's ecosystems.

In the late 1980s, I worked with a small team to represent patents and technologies in America for Japan's top inventor, Dr. Yoshiro Nakamatsu, who may have more patents than anyone in history. Aside from his more "out there" inventions that came into his eccentric mind, he had some very valuable innovations, potentially including a means to contain and clean up nuclear waste, which apparently was not a profit center and therefore not of much interest.

Representing Dr. Nakamatsu brought us into closer relationships with some interesting parties, including NASA Technology Transfer. Part of the mission of NASA and justification of the large budgets is to develop and deploy technologies funded by the government and cross them over into the public domain for use by mainstream American Business. I thought this exchange of technology was wonderful until I learned how NASA penetrating camera satellites were being rented and deployed by the commercial fishing industry to help fishing boats spot and track fish over 300 lb so that they could be efficiently caught. This and other examples showed how technology can be abused and used against the Earth and humanity.

I believe there are three perspectives on these types of controversial topics: 1) Those who intuit deeper truths and believe in their possibilities, 2) Those who do not believe and are opposed to such notions, and 3) Those who know but cannot disclose confidential information due to their Confidentiality Agreements with various intelligence agencies.

What is undeniably clear is that for whatever the underlying reasons, the unrelenting march of technological advancement and its applications for purposes, such as energy production or militarization of weapons of mass destruction has led us to the very brink of potential destruction. Technology is in the hands of those who wield it, and there are those who have their hands on various control buttons. Even non-military technology for industry and human comfort threatens the very equilibrium that sustains the planet's ecosystems and therefore humankind. One way or another, rapidly advancing technology has us standing on the edge of this precipice of a major course correction.

Here are a few specific ways technological advancements whisper signs of hope and danger:

Machine Conveniences: Transportation, air conditioning, refrigeration, and many other modern devices that make our lives more convenient and enjoyable consume massive amounts of energy, create pollution, and increase accident risks.

Energy Innovations: Advancements in harnessing renewable energy along with technologies supporting ecological regeneration offer glimpses of a more sustainable and equitable future. These innovations hold the potential to address pressing challenges like energy consumption and information access. However, these industries are making billions of dollars a day by selling us petroleum and nuclear power so they block and prevent alternative energy solutions from becoming available because it would hurt their own self-interests.

Automated Weaponry: While innovations in robotics and artificial intelligence can allow for remote military actions that may protect soldiers, automated weapons could also be turned upon military personnel and civilian populations by rogue actors. Many are aware that governments already possess drones and robotic military equipment, including state-level governments for their own population control imperatives.

Artificial Intelligence: AI stands as a testament to humanity's quest for knowledge, bringing tools to pierce the veil of complexity and attain insights previously unfathomable. However, most have also seen science-fiction scenarios of AI turning against people. More subtle risks like an AI writing inaccurate information also exist. What is not yet as broadly talked about is the massive number of existing jobs and positions that will soon be replaced by various AI systems that are more cost-effective. The resulting unemployment will create an even larger burden on the economy and public sector.

Genetic Manipulation: The direct alteration of an organism's genes to produce desirable traits, presents immense promise along with significant perils. While gene editing tools like CRISPR open possibilities for curing diseases, enhancing nutrition, and environmental remediation, they also pose risks of unintended consequences. Safety hazards for gene-edited crops and animals along with ethical concerns of genetically modified "designer babies" require deep consideration. Gene editing could irreversibly alter the human genome and the natural world in dangerous ways.

Quantum Sciences: Quantum theories reveal profound interconnectedness in existence, aligning with many spiritual traditions. Yet applications of quantum physics could also unlock new capabilities, forms even more dangerous than nuclear weapons if mishandled.

This crisis demands a profound paradigm shift. This transformative journey mandates a deep introspection of our collective and personal values, a critical examination of our actions, and most crucially, the commitment to align our needs with our deeds with increased understanding. Whether you feel ready or not for this transformation, it is right in front of us and will not be denied. The pain this crisis will cause is likely only going to increase until we manifest the changes and benefit from the shifts that will be required to modify our behavior and reverse the abuse of Spaceship Earth. These problems may be seen as outer manifestations of our collective policies and behavior, and an opportunity to express our divine nature and manifest our destiny as planetary caretakers.

In the following pages, we will explore the mechanisms for change in greater detail, examining the roots of our crises and potential solutions. We'll examine the current state of affairs, exploring how we might navigate this critical crossroads and emerge with technology working in a more harmonious way with an awakened Crew of Spaceship Earth.

The Urgency of a Paradigm Shift

Amidst the murmurings of change and the clamor for action, one reality stands starkly evident: the paradigm shift required is not a leisure option to be explored at our convenience. Instead, it is an urgent necessity that will accommodate no delay. Here, we outline some of the reasons that underscore its immediate urgency.

1. Accelerating Environmental Destabilization: Our planet's environmental balance is rapidly deteriorating and approaching catastrophic tipping points:

- Climate Change: Our dependence on fossil fuels and destruction of carbon sinks has disrupted the climate system, driving extreme weather, rising seas, and altering biomes. This destabilization leaves humanity exposed like astronauts without space suits.
- Mass Extinctions: Deforestation, overfishing, pollution, and unsustainable agriculture are annihilating biodiversity, and depleting nature's resilience. Up to 200 species go extinct daily.
- Resource Depletion: Dwindling resources like fossil fuels, rare earth minerals, and freshwater place severe strain on supply chains and global cooperation. Competition over scarce commodities may ignite conflicts.
- Toxic Buildup: Vast quantities of biological and industrial waste accumulate, poisoning ecosystems. Nuclear waste will need to be safely contained for millennia.

2. **Fraying Social Fabric:** Environmental degradation exacerbates societal divisions and unrest:

- Wealth Disparity: Economic imbalances worsen as resources decline, stoking public discontent. Elites profit from crises while most suffer.
- Leadership Vacuum: Governments downplay environmental threats, protecting business interests over citizens. This erodes public trust, already strained by partisanship.
- Supply Chain Disruptions: Global trade depends on stable agriculture, infrastructure, and energy systems. Disrupting these risks food shortages, deprivation, and unrest.

3. **Economic Implications:** Ignoring ecological limits eventually strains our growth-dependent economy:

- Market Shocks: Extreme weather, reduced resources, and supply chain disruptions create market volatility. Cascading impacts spread rapidly.
- Inequitable Impacts: Poorer regions have fewer buffers against resource scarcity, price spikes, disasters, and health threats. Inequality worsens.
- Delayed Action Amplifies Costs: Mitigating climate change and environmental damage becomes costlier over time. Early action is prudent risk management.

4. Existential Threats: Crossing environmental tipping points risks civilizational collapse:

- Climate Tipping Cascades: Feedback loops like melting permafrost and collapsing ice sheets trigger runaway warming once initiated.
- Mass Migration and Conflict: Climate impacts may displace over 1 billion people by 2050, challenging regional stability.
- Civilization Requires Ecological Stability: Food production, water cycles, and disease regulation all depend on the planetary equilibrium humanity is disrupting.

The Future We Risk: While the above realities are grim, they are not preordained. They underscore the importance of swift, decisive action. Every moment we delay our paradigm shift, we accrue a debt — one that future generations will be forced to repay, often with heart-wrenching interest.

Shifting now, albeit challenging, is akin to course-correcting a ship slightly off its path. Delaying might mean attempting a U-turn in turbulent waters, with waves of past inaction threatening to capsize our collective vessel.

The urgent call is clear: The time to recalibrate our trajectory, redefine our values, and embrace a sustainable paradigm is right now. Not in a decade, not tomorrow, but today. The future we stand to gain is one where Spaceship Earth thrives well into a distant future, safeguarded by a vigilant, compassionate crew that recognizes the interconnectivity of all life and is dedicated to its preservation.

Recognizing the Gem of God

I was raised in a conservative "Christian" family. We were among the few people on the planet that had salvation and all the facts pointed to this truth. It was a hardline religion that often made it difficult for me to feel comfortable. As a child, I wanted to express my love loudly and vigorously for God, but I was told not to sing in church because I sang loudly off-key. The first time I felt like I could truly express my love and devotion for God was with my Yogini Nanny Isabel, who showed me the gentle and accepting love of Allah. I did not know until many years later that Allah was not the same as the God that I grew up worshiping and he was Muslim. I found this very strange because I'd always considered them to be the same God and could not understand the difference, even how that was possible given they both are omni-everything.

I learned later how throughout history, religious and spiritual differences have often been a source of discord, wars, and separation. When I visited the various churches, I found their perspectives to almost always be aligned with mine. This is how I first came up with the Gem of God Theory.

Picture the facets on a diamond, each uniquely reflecting light yet all part of the same gem. They surround the gem, facing many different directions, together in any one direction representing a full 356 degrees of a circle. Like a gem, each religion offers its distinct viewpoint on the divine, like individual facets on a sacred gem. Every religion, like a face on a gem, has a flat surface and a well-defined edge.

From that observation point, there is a perfectly clear view inside of the gem. It must be the best and truest perspective possible!

Every spiritual tradition names the divine essence in its own tongue, yet they point to the same underlying mystery inside the gem. Allah, Jesus, Buddha, Krishna, Yahweh - these signify unique cultural portals to the formless infinite, much as facets direct light in unique ways into a diamond's depth. The direction of the facets may differ significantly when looking at the whole stone. They can even be 180 degrees different, where the direction of inside and away from the stone is literally 180 different in completely opposite directions. Yet when the reference is relative to the face of the stone, they all function in the same way. Although derived from diverse cultures, they share the intent of connecting finite minds with the infinite spirit, like light entering a gem. Doctrines and dogmas are intellectual attempts to grasp the ultimately ineffable nature of God, explaining different properties of the sacred gem.

If looking from a greater perspective it is clear that none can legitimately claim their religion fully encapsulates the entirety of the Divine. However, from their seat, the view seems so perfect. How could a single facet reveal the whole gem? This is one of the great mysteries of the Creator. Even deeply personal experiences that are directed only at our own single view can seem world-changing, like it should be shouted from the mountain tops. Our understanding is limited, yet the transcendent truth shines boundlessly beyond words or concepts permeating our being.

Recognizing this, we can relinquish arrogant claims of exclusive ownership of Truth. Our beliefs may be guideposts, but not rigid dogmas. They invite exploration. Seeing unity beneath diversity fosters interfaith dialogue. Shared values become evident across traditions. As with facets on a gem, the angles and direction up may be different than any other position, but they all emanate from the same center. Each religion reflects a unique way the Divine manifests in culture, time, and geography, like pure light refracted into distinct colors. Yet, the essence remains one, like white light containing the entire spectrum. Beneath exoteric differences lies the Universal Spirit and Truth. By focusing on this common spiritual core, we can transcend divisions.

When we focus on the unifying core of spiritual traditions, a universal ethos emerges. An ethos centered on devotion to the welfare of all creatures, reverence for life's sanctity, and faith in divine benevolence. From this shared ground, a collective understanding of our duty to creation unfolds — to propagate consciously, not recklessly; to live in balance, not domination.

Unity, not uniformity, is key to manifesting this ethos. Each tradition lends its unique wisdom, while believing in shared responsibility. Then sustainable existence aligns with spiritual values. As facets on a gem, varied beliefs reveal glimpses of divinity. Together, we can revere life's divine spark and hopefully prevent a global ecological collapse.

Prophecies of Change

This pivotal planetary transformation is not an unforeseen event. Adepts have seen this coming for a long time and now it is just on our doorstep. For ages, humans have held a fascination with the future and its potential for change. This theme has influenced many cultures and spiritual traditions that have prophesied about a massive, looming transformation that will fundamentally alter the nature of human existence. From the Mayan civilization and Indigenous tribes of North America to the philosophical traditions of Christianity, Buddhism, and Islam, we can see how this anticipated great change is integrated into our collective consciousness.

Mayan Calendar

The ancient Mayans, an advanced civilization that thrived in Mesoamerica for centuries, are renowned for their sophisticated understanding of astronomy and time. Their intricate calendar system, consisting of several interlocking cycles, has generated much intrigue and speculation, particularly around the concept of the "end of the world."

The Mayans tracked time through a 260-day sacred calendar (Tzolkin) and a 365-day solar calendar (Haab'), which intersected every 52 years to form a "Calendar Round." However, they also recognized a broader cycle called the "Long Count," a period of 5,125 years.

While some have interpreted the completion of a Long Count cycle as a prediction of an apocalyptic end, Mayan scholars argue that it signifies the end of one era and the beginning of a new one, a time of transformation and renewal. It's less about catastrophe and more about evolution and marks the beginning of a new era of consciousness and spiritual awakening.

Axis Mundi

The concept of the Axis Mundi, or the world's center, is a pervasive element across many religious and mythological traditions. In this context, the Axis Mundi is not a physical location but a spiritual concept, representing the journey of spiritual growth, transformation, and the cyclical nature of existence. It speaks to a process of continual renewal, where the old gives way to the new, providing the conditions for growth and evolution. It has symbolized the connection and shift between the earthly and the divine and an impending climax of a global cycle of the death of one way and subsequent rebirth into a new way.

Native American Prophecies

Numerous Native American tribes share prophecies that foretell a time of great change and renewal. One of the most well-known is the prophecy of the Seventh Generation, attributed to various tribes, which states that a time will come when the decisions made by the current generation will significantly affect the survival and well-being of seven generations into the future.

Hopi Prophecy of the "Blue Star Kachina."

Hopi legends speak of a transformative era signaled by the appearance of a blue star. Some believe this symbol being actualized by the advent of seeing Earth as a blue star from space. The following period, described is a time of purification, through a period of turmoil, and then to a new age of peace and unity among all peoples.

Christian Prophecies

Christianity has its own prophecies of transformative change. The Book of Revelation, the final book of the New Testament, is filled with prophetic visions that depict a period of tribulation, followed by the arrival of a new heaven and a new earth. While interpretations vary widely, many see this as a metaphor for a radical shift in human consciousness and societal structures. The old ways must pass away, making room for a new era of peace, justice, and unity.

Buddhist Prophecies

Buddhist traditions also speak of future change. In particular, the notion of Maitreya, a future Buddha who will achieve complete enlightenment and teach pure dharma, signals an era of spiritual awakening and transformation. The advent of Maitreya is believed to usher in a time when the teachings of the Buddha will be forgotten, only to be rediscovered and spread across the world, facilitating a global shift in consciousness.

Islamic Prophecies

In Islamic tradition, there are Hadiths — sayings of the Prophet Muhammad — that reference the arrival of a figure known as the Mahdi, a redeemer who will rule before the Day of Judgment and, alongside Jesus, will bring justice and peace to the world. Like other prophecies, this foretells a period of great upheaval followed by renewal and change.

Some believe Christ, Maitreya and Mahdi to be referencing the same being or collective dynamic of God consciousness. These prophecies, despite their different origins and while varying in detail and imagery, converge on a shared theme: a period of time where the inevitability of massive change climaxes into a transformative resolution.

These prophecies, despite their different origins, share a vision of cyclical change and rebirth. Whether foretold as the end of an era, the coming of a savior, or a shift in global consciousness, all of these prophecies from many different cultures and time periods around the world predict a massive change as a fundamental step onto the next level of our existence. As passengers and now the crew of this spaceship we call Earth, we are part of this grand cycle, both influenced by it and influencers within it. Together, we journey toward a future that dances with potential destruction, yet holds the promise of renewal, evolution, and opportunity for profound growth.

II.
Turning Crisis into Opportunity

As we stand at this crossroads, shifting from peril to potential is far from a guaranteed outcome. We are at a proverbial O.K. Corral of our hopes for a brighter future, where the established power structures seem overpowering, while our poor conditioning confuses our natural sense of self-preservation. Many are paralyzed in fear or distraction, diluting their ability to navigate their basic challenges, let alone envision the initiatives for positive transformation of the powerful internal and external crises we face.

However, let's draw inspiration from the Chinese ideogram for crisis "weiji," which melds the symbols for danger ("wei") and opportunity ("ji"). We need to recognize that every crisis carries within it the seed for transformation. This perspective not only highlights the imminent dangers we face but also underscores the inherent transformative potential embedded within our current challenges. In the realm of Change Management, there's a prevailing axiom — People typically resist change until the discomfort of their current state surpasses the apprehension of the impending change. Once they accept the change, they tend to adapt fairly quickly if given clear direction. It is up to the

Visionary leaders and artists to offer vision with clear direction, yet, we must also be careful to not create an angry stampede, even if it appears to be going in the right direction. We must seek to engender contemplative cohesion, but not mob-unconsciousness.

Turning our current crisis into opportunity necessitates accepting the necessity of the change and establishing plans with clear direction. This transformative journey mandates a profound paradigm shift starting with a deep introspection of our values, a critical examination of our actions, and most crucially, the commitment to align our needs with our deeds with increased understanding. It beckons us to reassemble the fragments of our dispersed identities, amalgamating them into cohesive, centered beings with clarity of purpose.

I know some people who might react to this idea with "Do you know what planet you are on?" Yet, it seems commonly believed by many hard-working Americans that the students from an average high school would be able to manage the country better than the President, Congress, and Senate. I definitely believe they would make better macro-decisions that are more directly aligned to resolve the actual issues we face. Not because they are smarter, but because they are not primarily serving special interest campaign donors or other hidden alliances.

More than ever, we must now commune to operate as a unified crew, guiding Spaceship Earth toward a future defined by our higher sensibilities, which naturally recognize the need for ecological sustainability and social equity.

Despite the immense challenges we face, I still have hope. In my life, I've glimpsed a hint of something I consider "divine," dormant wisdom and goodness within most people, though it often lays buried beneath layers of conditioning and distraction. I believe that if we come together unified by a shared vision and values, we can awaken this latent potential within ourselves and others. Through collective introspection and conscious choice, we can tap into our innate sensibilities that recognize the need for ecological sustainability, social equity, and unity. More than ever, we must commune and cooperate as an awakened crew guiding our planetary vessel toward a future that honors life in all its forms and transforms this time of tribulation into an era that uplifts our higher humanity.

Cyclical and Linear Time

Throughout human existence, our perception and interpretation of time have played pivotal roles in how we think and behave. The shift from Cyclical Time to Linear Time is one of the most profound transitions in human history. It has been made manifest in two predominant periods of perceptual evolution: First, there was Cyclical Time and then Linear Time, which has come into predominance. Each mode holds its unique influence over societies, economies, religions, and personal lives, shaping them in subtle and overt ways. The deep-rooted implications of these perspectives, once untangled, provide an illuminating lens to view the challenges we face.

The shift to Linear Time has more than just affected our perception of time, it has left indelible footprints on our cultural goals, religions, social structures, political agendas, economies, and relationships with the environment. Much of the uncertainty we face today, along with our difficulty in navigating toward a more promising and sustainable future, can be illuminated by understanding the implications of this dynamic. The pressing issues of our current era — such as climate change, social inequality, economic instability, and a collective sense of disconnection — cannot be fully grasped without comprehending our journey from cyclical to linear time perspectives, and their respective consequences.

Echoes from Nature's cycles and our ancestors' profound observations of the world around them birthed the understanding of the patterns of cyclical time. Witnessing nature's myriad cycles- the consistent rhythm of seasons, the predictable pattern of the moon's phases, the sun's faithful rise and set, the time to plant and harvest, the migration of animals, the time to hunker down for winter are all patterns that repeat year in and year out. These annual patterns helped our ancestors to understand time as a series of recurrent, interlocking circles. This understanding of time led to the creation of calendars based on lunar or solar cycles, planting, and harvesting schedules tied to the seasons, and community celebrations and rituals that marked these cyclical changes. These patterns were so much a part of our foundational understanding of life that they are intrinsically embedded into our DNA, our deepest levels of the psyche, and patterns of behavior.

In the cyclical worldview, humans are one of the threads in the vast tapestry of holistic existence. The notion fostered a deep respect for every living entity, knowing that each had its role in the larger ballet of life. By observing the Earth's rhythm, we synchronized our existence, from agriculture to religious ceremonies, and we strove to be in harmony with the timing of the natural world that cradled and nurtured us. These cycles helped keep us grounded and close to the earth, aware of how nature meets our survival needs. We tend to her, and she provides for us. The more we sow, the more we reap. It is the natural order of life- of circular time.

While cyclical time painted a harmonious picture, the emergence of linear time — characterized by a belief in "salvation" with goals defined in a beginning, middle, and end — introduced a different dynamic. Birthed from scientific, industrial, religious, and capitalist revolutions, this perspective shifted our view to a structured progression of events, each following the other around the notion we can make life better and bring nature more under our control.

While linear time and progress have led to some remarkable advancements, this headlong march into the future has often come at the expense of our bond with nature's rhythms. We have become a society obsessed with advancement, seldom pausing to align our relentless pace with the circular cycles of nature governing our own environments.

Cyclical time does not merely dictate a worldview but also a balanced growth view. In societies grounded in natural ways growth is not some limitless surge forward, but it is a harmonious dance of progression and regression. Such a rhythm inculcated values of gratitude, conservation, and reciprocity. The modern notion of 'deficit living' that we have called "progress" for the last few hundred years, taking whatever we want from the Earth's endless supply without tending her, is coming soon to a screeching halt. It is a bankrupt enterprise. We literally have consumed billions of years of energy stored in the Earth's bioenergetic battery over the last 100 years with little to show for it but environmental damage — a dawning reality coming home to roost with a vengeance.

As Strauss and Howe elucidate in *The Fourth Turning*, society began arranging itself around linear generational archetypes. Each generation became a stepping stone, leading the next towards what was envisioned as the next step of progress. But herein lay a paradox: while this linear progression aims for continual advancement, it often overlooks the essential cyclical rhythms that govern our world and defines progress or advancement as shimmying out further on the limb, climbing higher in altitude onto branches that cannot support our weight.

Endless progression led us down a road of relentless consumption, unconstrained growth, and, inadvertently, ecological disregard. We became participants in the "Mad Race To Nowhere," sacrificing long-term sustainability for perceived short-term gain. The consequence of this mad race that has goals in conflict with our true nature is evident in our fraying relationship with the environment and the increasing societal disparities.

It seems completely evident that the direction needed to move back into harmony with the fundamentals of life requires us to rekindle an appreciation for the rhythms and reciprocal ways of nature, focused within our own immediate geographic setting. Realigning our lives into harmony with the cycles of our local food supply, the seasons, and the knowledge embedded in the earth around us, will not only help us strike a new balance between innovation and sustainability, but it will also help us center into our ancestral core of being programmed over millions of years, nurturing our peace of mind and sense of order.

Re-Embracing Cyclical Patterns

The dance between cyclical and linear time, nature and technological societies is intricate. While each perspective offers its unique insights; with cyclical time anchoring us to nature's rhythm and linear time propelling us towards envisioned progress, our journey ahead demands a harmonious integration of the two. It beckons for a future where our definition of progress is one that harmonizes our lifestyles and society with nature and her rhythms, ensuring our world thrives both in spirit and in substance.

We have a greater capacity than ever before to change our trajectory by honoring circular patterns and realigning our communities with the natural flows of life. Although the chasm between linear and cyclical time seems vast, each of us has the power to build bridges, whether through our lifestyle choices, educational priorities, or community-building efforts. What empowers us to bridge this chasm between linear and cyclical time?

First, our advanced cognition allows us to comprehend time in deeper ways. We can consciously grasp the nuances of cyclical and linear perspectives, understanding their pros and cons. This meta-awareness of time perception is unique to our species and has expanded with our vastly expanded access to knowledge of every variety.

Second, we have developed extensive collaborations, communication networks, and knowledge banks that enable large-scale coordination. This collective intelligence means insights can spread rapidly, driving cultural change through shared revelations.

Third, our innovations in education, media, and community development give us tools to practically shift mindsets and behaviors. Curriculum reforms, awareness campaigns, urban agriculture, and seasonal rituals allow the practical integration of circular wisdom into daily life.

Fourth, our innate creativity provides the vision to redesign systems and societies along natural principles. We can imagine outside the box of linear progression and status quo. Our art and culture seed visions of more cyclical living that help bend the arc of progress.

Fifth, our capacity for complex analysis, scenario planning, and modeling with tools such as AI allows us to carefully recalibrate systems rather than drastically disrupt them. We can judiciously re-introduce circular elements while innovating new syntheses.

While the divide may seem unbridgeable from our conditioned perspective, our combined capacities for wisdom, cooperation, innovation, creativity, and thoughtful systems change empower us to consciously build new spans, uniting the best of cyclical and linear time into a sustainable future. When grounded in nature's wisdom, our gifts uplift both current and coming generations.

Our future flourishing hinges on synthesizing technological progress with ecological balance. To address the chasm between these two perspectives, we are working on new models for intentional communities and modern villages that incorporate the wisdom inherent in cyclical rhythms and strive to innovate ways to restore lifestyles that are in balance with natural ways of living, such as those shared in the section of this book, *Reintegrating Village Wisdom.*

Visionaries across eras have long foreseen the very juncture we navigate, prophesying a great transformation that ultimately realigns humanity's trajectory with the natural order. From the ancients who crafted intricate calendars tracking cosmic cycles to mystics who spoke of transcending earthly duality, our ancestors whisper that the linear march of progress cannot continue unchecked forever. Indigenous tribes prophesied a shift catalyzed by Earth's upheaval. The unwavering faith that we would one day reincorporate cyclical insights allowed societies to record their wisdom, knowing future generations would require it to right their course after straying astray.

Now, as we witness the limits of linearity in our chaotic lives and social fragmentation, we should not be overly caught off guard since the insights of prophets past and present have predicted this moment of change. Let's now dredge up a few nuggets of timeless knowledge from humanity's vaults and brush them off for review.

Learning from Cultural Wisdom

I came from a traditionally conditioned American upbringing, where we believed that technology and modern medicine reigned supreme. Our good God and Jesus have provided us with the world for our taking, like some giant supermarket, well stocked with every other living creature as our products and consumables. This was our divine right, to take whatever we want whenever we choose and discard the rest. To just throw it away, out of sight, so someone else can deal with it. I was the product of a capitalistic system, 'Living the Life' in a free market economy that could solve any problem better and more efficiently than any other system the world has ever known. Yes, I was fully acculturated, completely deluded, and a good American.

I thank God and the mysterious nature of life that I was led early into the company of other very different cultures. When I was 12 years old, my parents separated and moved apart: I moved from La Jolla to North Park in San Diego, where my mother met and hired a neighbor to be our part-time nanny so that she could work a job. My new nanny, Isabel, turned out to be a 10th-generation Yogi from Pakistan, as was her husband. They lived in a Kriya Yoga commune adjacent to our new, much smaller home.

I had been born with inadequate immunities. It was a condition that our doctor saw absolutely no correlation to my mother being fed copious quantities of antibiotics when she was pregnant or the continuation of the plan, which kept me on antibiotics my entire childhood like they were daily vitamins. My doctor explained that my health was just a natural disaster on its own due to my genetics. For my first 12 years, I had never breathed without my lungs bubbling, and I had sinus headaches almost every day that felt like hot spikes were driven through my forehead.

Isabel led me to start practicing yoga daily. She gave me Ayurvedic herbs and taught me healing techniques. Within about 90 days, my health was restored, and I was living pain-free for the first time in my life. She also opened my eyes and set me on a path to appreciate the natural world and other Indigenous cultures. While I moved away and lost touch with her a few years later, I cannot possibly thank her enough for what she has contributed to my growth and life path.

Isabel revealed to me that every culture, across continents and eons, has been a wellspring of wisdom. As she explained, the very fact that anyone is alive is proof that their specific ancestral lineage has existed, unbroken since the beginning of life and time. She helped me cultivate practices and philosophies that echoed the principles of sustainable living, deep community ties, and harmony with the natural world, which she revealed is full of deep and profound mysteries. Much of what I learned with Isabel about various cultures and life's mysteries I cannot help but share because they are so deeply embedded in who I am now and are relevant to our transformation and challenge.

The adage, "history repeats itself," serves as a poignant reminder that unless we heed the lessons of the past, we risk repeating them. While many of our present challenges are unprecedented in scope and complexity, they are not entirely detached from the trials and tribulations of our ancestors. Nor are our challenges immune to the natural and grounded remedies that worked in ages gone by. At their core, our crisis issues arise from an imbalance — a deviation from the intricate equilibrium that once maintained human civilization's balanced relationship with nature and one another.

In the relentless rush of modern life, we have become increasingly disconnected from ancient wisdom. But as the pressures of climate imbalance, social inequality, and technological disruption converge, there's a growing awareness and urgent imperative to bridge the gap between our rich heritage and our contemporary predicaments.

Some of the more fortunate people are instinctively drawn to their roots and the wisdom of Indigenous cultures, sensing they hold some form of positive magic for them. Other people resort to relying upon what they are told are scientific breakthroughs, sterile environments, bold detergents, modern medicine, and the conveyances in our disposable, plug-and-play lifestyle. In my opinion, many of these advancements of our modern age and lifestyle clearly lead in the wrong direction. My travels have shown me that people living in far more primitive environments with less material goods and technology are actually happier people who appreciate what little they have.

The key isn't to regress or romanticize the past but to distill its essence and extract those timeless principles that promoted balance, resilience, and mutual respect and weave them into the fabric of our modern societies. By looking closely at what has worked for generations in the past, we stand a better chance of protecting our own future. We can integrate many profound insights and techniques of our ancestors, how they survived and flourished over many generations of time, and weave them with the boundless possibilities of tomorrow.

Modern scientific theories also hint at this innate bond between life and nature. The Gaia Hypothesis, conceptualized by scientist James Lovelock, suggests the Earth functions as a self-regulating system where organisms and surroundings interact to maintain conditions for life. Lovelock named it after the Greek Earth goddess Gaia. While debated, the theory reinforces Indigenous intuitions of an interconnected web of existence, where all components synergize towards balance. Just as Indigenous cultures understood their intricate relationship with nature, the Gaia framework sees the Earth as more than just a passive host to life, but rather an interconnected, symbiotic ecosystem that is also a macro-lifeform.

As we excavate deeper into the realm of cultural wisdom, we'll examine some Indigenous knowledge systems that have long championed a balanced and harmonious way of life. We will understand the importance of communal living, embodied by the age-old concept of the village. We'll rediscover the value of self-sufficiency, not just as a means of survival but as a path to meaningful existence. Through these lenses, we'll also discern how to perpetuate skills and strengthen community bonds in an era where both seem to be eroding.

But our journey won't be limited to gazing into the rearview mirror. We'll also turn our sights forward, drawing inspiration from futuristic cultural models that hold keys to evolving. By amalgamating the old with the new, we weave a unique fabric, empowering us to nurture a more enlightened, sustainable, and interconnected world.

Models for Creating Balance and Harmony

As we venture into the exploration of various models of balance and harmony that have factored into the models proposed in this book, I wish to point out that these models, whether ancient wisdom traditions or modern scientific disciplines, may deserve deeper exploration than I will provide within this book. Many of them hold potential keys to unlocking a sustainable and harmonious future for our planet and I encourage our readers to study further any models that resonate and call to them. In the following pages, we synthesize the essence of these diverse systems, focusing on their common themes and most salient points rather than providing comprehensive expositions of any.

Blue Zones Project

I believe the Blue Zones Project deserves a special mention among my list since, in my opinion, it is a true manifestation of an evolutionary system amidst the challenges we face. Dan Buettner's life work creating the Blue Zones Project stands as a beacon of hope, demonstrating that it is possible to create thriving, resilient communities. Blue Zones are regions around the world where people live exceptionally long and healthy lives, often reaching the age of 100 at rates up to 10 times higher than the average population. I believe he has also evolved a brilliant formula to naturally align modern people with the natural order of life by appealing to their own desire to live longer more fulfilling lives.

These are some of the models that have influenced my vision, beginning with the deep-rooted wisdom of Indigenous cultures and leading into the future from around the world. They include:

Indigenous Tribal Wisdom

We explore the practices and philosophies of some insightful Indigenous tribal cultures worldwide. Their deep connection with nature and emphasis on community over individualism can provide valuable lessons on achieving balance and harmony.

Modern Tribal Paradigms

In the contemporary world, the concept of "tribe" has evolved and transcended its traditional meaning and boundaries. Today's tribes are not solely defined by ethnic or Indigenous identities. Modern tribes, formed around shared beliefs, values, or experiences, are emerging as potent societal units, fostering deep connections among members. These tribal societies showcase their unique models of cultural sharing, balance, harmony, and sustainability. Their ways of tribal interaction and identification are deeply rooted in aspects of who they are and bonding with others who share their common vision and need to respect what they value.

In essence, both ancient tribal models and the emerging modern tribal paradigms underline the profound human need for connection, collaboration, and community. By studying and integrating their principles, we can create more balanced, harmonious, and inclusive societies in our increasingly globalized world.

Village Models

Villages in the Middle Ages, such as the English village of Elton, often functioned around the concept of a commons where resources were shared and stewardship was communal. The guild system, which included apprenticeships, journeyman phases, and mastery, ensured the passing down of crafts and skills and created a balance between education, work, and community involvement.

Intentional Communities

Intentional communities are modern iterations of the village model and can take many forms. Communities such as the Findhorn Foundation in Scotland or the Twin Oaks Community in Virginia, USA, intentionally organize their lives around shared values of cooperation, sustainability, and mutual care. These models demonstrate that societies built around common intention can thrive and offer valuable alternative models to mainstream culture.

Eco-villages

I have lived within intentional ecological communities for years and have found them to benefit my health and EQ (Emotional Intelligence Quotient). These are often based on sustainable principles and permaculture designs. While living in the previous community, I made and tended huge worm bins to generate worm tea, which was all of the organic fertilizer needed for our organic garden and orchards. For years, I collected coffee grounds and compost daily from restaurants in the surrounding area to make compost and fertile topsoil. Let me say I got my hands well into the soil and loved it.

Eastern Philosophies

Philosophies such as Yin-Yang in Chinese philosophy, Dharma in Hinduism, or the Middle Way in Buddhism highlight the necessity of balance, the acceptance of change, and harmony with the self and the world.

Spiritual Teachings

Many spiritual traditions, including mystic Christianity, Sufism, Kabbalah, and Taoism, emphasize the interconnection and unity of all life and teach practices for living in harmony with this fundamental reality.

Permaculture Principles

Permaculture integrates land, resources, people, and the environment through mutually beneficial synergies. Its ethical foundation of Earth care, people care, and fair share formulates a philosophy of working with, rather than against nature.

Holistic Health Models

The biopsychosocial model in health care emphasizes an integrated approach considering the physical, psychological, and social factors playing a role in health and illness. Its principles can be expanded to the health of societies and the planet.

Environmental Activism

Activists unite organized efforts by concerned citizens, often through non-profit organizations or grassroots movements to protect the natural world. Activism creates a sense of community while it brings critical environmental issues to light and advocates for policies and behaviors that support ecological sustainability.

Circular Economies

This model can help us move from our current "take, make, dispose" linear economy to a "borrow, use, return, recycle, redeploy" system, imitating natural cycles where tools and items are kept in use and waste becomes a resource for new cycles of growth.

Non-Profit Organizations

I founded a non-profit, Nature's Blueprint, which proposes that the "Word of God" is embedded in the natural world and shared through various languages, such as genetics, physics, mathematics, dendrochronology (the study of tree rings), and other natural expressions that hold solutions to many of the dilemmas we face. It promotes initiatives such as preserving the living genetic diversity of all plant and animal species; the collection and redeployment of human waste and biomass without heavy metals to return back into soil and fertility cycles to help reverse desertification, as one demonstration of how society can be realigned to support, rather than undermine, the intricate balances and harmonies of nature.

Systems Theory

This scientific discipline offers models for understanding how complex systems, like societies or ecosystems, maintain balance and harmony. Concepts like homeostasis, feedback loops, and emergent properties could help us comprehend how the imbalances in our current systems have arisen and how we can rectify them.

Change Management

We can hardly discuss models of balance and harmony without considering how to manage and adapt to the pain of change. The change management model, as articulated by visionary industry leader, and friend, Daryl Conner, founder of the eminent consulting firm, Connor Partners, and author of *Managing at the Speed of Change* and *Leading At The Edge of Chaos*, provides crucial insights in this realm. Conner's work provides valuable tools to anticipate and facilitate change as well as navigate resistance to it. He offers methodologies for guiding transformative processes before they reach unbearable thresholds of pain. In this way, change management can serve the process of navigating the turbulent seas of transition to reach the safer shores of a more sustainable and harmonious future.

These historical and modern models, local and global, provided me with diverse blueprints for organizing human societies in sustainable, equitable, and harmonious ways. They serve as guiding lights on my journey to conceptualizing Activating The Crew of Spaceship Earth. Let us now look a bit deeper into a few aspects of these models.

Blue Zones Project

Dan Buettner, founder of the Blue Zones project, is the author of several books on the topic, including "The Blue Zones: Lessons for Living Longer from the People Who've Lived the Longest" and "The

Blue Zones Solution: Eating and Living Like the World's Healthiest People." I highly recommend learning more about his team's work.

Buettner's interest in longevity and health began when he was working as a journalist for National Geographic. He led a series of expeditions to study the world's longest-lived populations, which he termed "Blue Zones." His team consisted of demographers, anthropologists, epidemiologists, and other researchers who studied the lifestyle habits and environmental factors contributing to the exceptional longevity in these regions. Through this work, Buettner has discovered a theme for balanced living that serves as an example of how life can and must work in harmony with nature, both our own and the planet's.

While Buettner's focus is on improving the health of people, it is clear to me that his philosophy is a prime example that what is good for people can and must also be good for the health of the planet. The suggested lifestyles in Blue Zones minimize damage to the environment and emphasize natural health and time-honored traditions of honoring the Earth's vitality. By adopting these principles, we not only enhance our own well-being but also contribute to the healing and preservation of our planet.

After publishing his findings, Buettner founded the Blue Zones project, a community-based initiative to help cities and towns across the United States adopt the healthy lifestyle principles observed in the original Blue Zones. The project collaborates with local governments, schools, employers, and other community organizations to implement changes in the environment, policies, and social networks that make healthy choices more accessible for residents.

The Blue Zones project has been successful in improving health outcomes and lowering healthcare costs in participating communities. Buettner's work has inspired people worldwide to adopt healthier lifestyle habits and has contributed to a growing understanding of the factors that promote health and longevity, while simultaneously fostering a deeper connection to the natural world. His formula appeals to most people from many walks of life and philosophies because it is a universal desire for healthy humans to want to live longer, and more fulfilling lives.

Indigenous Wisdom

Indigenous cultures, having lived in close communion with nature for millennia, hold lessons that are deeply relevant today. Their ways of life emphasize the significance of symbiotic relationships, respect for the land, and community cooperation.

- **Respect and Reverence for Nature:** Indigenous societies have an inherent understanding that Earth is not just a resource but a living entity deserving of respect and gratitude. By treating the environment, animals, and plants as sacred entities, they engender reverence, and economical use and replenish what they take with sustainable practices.
- **Holistic Living:** Their worldview often doesn't compartmentalize life into separate domains but sees the group as an interconnected web where every person's contributions are necessary and valuable, as well as their

actions having consequences that ripple through the community and environment.

These various Indigenous cultures, scattered across all continents, have evolved specific wisdom to help them thrive in an array of habitats, from lush rainforest to arid desert to icy tundra. Their survival and flourishing depended on the intricate knowledge of their environment, a deep reverence for the natural world, and the fostering of sustainable practices that ensure the health of both their communities and the ecosystems they inhabit.

Reflect upon the traditional practices of the **San people of Southern Africa,** who have long understood the importance of managing resources for the collective good. Their hunter-gatherer lifestyle, based on taking only what is needed and sharing generously within the community, presents a stark contrast to the contemporary culture of overconsumption.

Or the **Kogi people of Colombia**, who see themselves as the "Elder Brothers" of humanity, with a sacred duty to maintain the balance of the Earth. Their concept of "Aluna," an interconnected consciousness that binds all living things, reflects a profound understanding of ecology long before the term was coined in Western science.

The **Aymara people of the Andes** developed a highly efficient agricultural system that capitalized on the mountainous topography. Their method of constructing terraced fields, known as "Andenes," not only enabled the cultivation of a diverse range of crops but also reduced soil erosion and water runoff. This traditional technique continues to offer viable solutions for sustainable farming in mountainous regions today.

The **Maasai of East Africa,** renowned for their pastoralist lifestyle, have developed systems of rotational grazing that preserve the vitality of their grasslands, preventing overgrazing and soil erosion. Their philosophy of "Enkai," a divine force linking all living beings, underpins their commitment to sustainability and harmony with nature.

Or the **Kayapó people of the Amazon Rainforest**, whose understanding of their environment has led to the preservation of large sections of the rainforest. The Kayapó have practiced a form of shifting cultivation that promotes biodiversity, clears undergrowth to prevent devastating wildfires, and regenerates the soil.

The **Aka People who reside in Central Africa**, often called the forest people, prioritize communal living and cooperation. Their hunter-gatherer lifestyle emphasizes equal sharing of resources, a stark contrast to many modern societies. Interestingly, they also exemplify gender equality, with men and women participating equally in hunting, gathering, and child-rearing.

We can also turn our attention to the **Indigenous Australians**, who for more than 60,000 years have lived with the rhythms of their environment, skillfully managing their resources through practices like "fire-stick farming", which reduces the risk of catastrophic bushfires and encourages biodiversity. They developed "Dreamtime" stories conveying complex ecological knowledge, embedding lessons of sustainable practices within their rich oral traditions. These narratives provided instructions for maintaining the land, managing resources, and respecting all forms of life.

Consider, for example, the **Native American tribes of the Great Plains**, whose buffalo-centered economies were sustainable models of resource usage. Every part of the buffalo was used — meat for food, skins for clothing and shelter, bones for tools — embodying a philosophy of complete utilization and minimal waste. This stands in stark contrast to our modern society where single-use plastics, fast fashion, and e-waste have become ubiquitous symbols of a throw-away culture.

The Haudenosaunee Confederacy, also known as the Iroquois Confederacy in North America, the Haudenosaunee represents a sophisticated system of socio-political governance. Their Great Law of Peace, predating the United States Constitution, is a powerful document that emphasizes peace, power, and righteousness. The Haudenosaunee values consensus in decision-making, ensuring every voice is heard, and having a profound respect for the natural world.

Look to the **tribes of the Pacific Northwest Coast, like the Haida and Tlingit**, whose potlatch system demonstrated a unique economic model of wealth distribution and social equilibrium. Instead of accumulating wealth, status was gained through the act of giving. This culture of reciprocity instilled community cohesion and a sense of shared responsibility for communal welfare.

Many Indigenous cultures, including numerous Native American tribes, have upheld a philosophy that perceives generosity and the act of giving as a sign of wealth and status, contrasting starkly with the more mainstream views of accumulation and possessions being associated with affluence. Those today who have amassed huge fortunes would likely have been pitied in those cultures for being poor in spirit and seeking to fill their inner void with too many possessions.

Wetiko is a term used in some Indigenous North American cultures, particularly among the Cree and Ojibwa peoples, to describe a destructive mindset of excessive greed and consumption. In the wetiko worldview, some individuals or societies lose sight of the sacred interconnectedness of all living beings in pursuit of their own self-interest. Much like an evil spirit that possesses a person, wetiko can take hold of both individuals and collectives, feeding endless cravings that ultimately hurt communities, nature, and the self. The notion of wetiko provides a lens for examining the costs of an economic order that rewards excess and extreme individualism while ignoring its impacts on the common good.

Among Indigenous cultures, tribes like the Lakota, Dakota, and Nakota (often collectively referred to as the Sioux) upheld a concept known as "wacantognaka," roughly translated as "generosity" or "the feeling of being generous." This principle wasn't just about giving in material terms but also pertained to showing kindness, sharing wisdom, and offering assistance. In these societies, the individual considered the most affluent wasn't the one who hoarded the most resources or had the most horses but rather the one who contributed the most to the community. An individual's reputation and standing within the tribe were often based on their ability to give away and share resources rather than accumulating them. Those who hoarded were seen as impoverished in spirit, lacking in the virtues these cultures held in high esteem. For example, a traditional Sioux ceremony called "give-away" was an occasion where individuals would distribute their possessions among the community, enhancing their social status. It underscored the idea that wealth doesn't come from what we keep but from what we give away. This Indigenous perspective offers a compelling counter-narrative to the modern capitalist notion of wealth and accumulation. It promotes a sense of community, shared responsibility, and a deep understanding of sustainability, demonstrating that one's prosperity shouldn't come at the expense of others or the environment.

Each of these examples illuminates a profound truth: sustainability is not a novel concept born out of modern environmentalism but an ancient wisdom born of necessity and reverence for the Earth. These cultures teach us that human beings are not separate from nature but an integral part of it. However, we need to recognize that these practices and knowledge systems cannot be separated from the cultures and peoples themselves. They are deeply rooted in specific social structures, spiritual beliefs, and traditional lifestyles. We can learn from how their practices emphasize respect, reciprocity, and relationship, principles that we must incorporate into our own societies if we hope to navigate the challenges of the 21st century.

Modern societies should recognize Indigenous people as equal partners in our journey towards a sustainable future, their rights acknowledged, and their sovereignty upheld.

Indigenous wisdom is not merely a resource to be tapped but a call to fundamentally transform our relationship with the Earth. Many of their time-honored traditions are the result of living locally, in contrast to America's modern grocery system where the food products travel an average of over 1200 miles to arrive on the Shelf.

Adapting to living in a more integrated fashion with the local environment not only reduces the risks inherent in large-scale system breakdowns, it also creates cultural diversification that enriches communities and brings out the unique qualities within various cultures that extend from our various geographic areas. This alignment is a journey of not just understanding, but of reacquainting and reintegrating a localized culture truly in harmony with our land. It honors our place in the natural world, developing our humility and increasing our respect, while embodying the profound wisdom that comes from our own deeper nature.

Now let's explore the depth from the deep well of the future and specific ways we can draw and apply these insights into our present-day challenges. Together, we are destined to forge a path that honors the wisdom of the past while being shaped by a futuristic vision.

Looking Forward into Culture

Embracing cultural wisdom is not just about looking back in time. Some futuristic models in literature and the visions of forward-thinkers present invaluable insights. As the adage goes, "The science fiction of today often becomes the reality of tomorrow." Time and again, this has held true: many notions once dismissed as mere flights of fancy now permeate our daily lives. While science fiction has an uncanny knack for forecasting real-world advancements, it also serves as a vital mirror, reflecting both the promise and perils of innovation. Offering glimpses of possible futures equips us with the foresight to embrace the benefits and sidestep potential pitfalls as we chart the course of progress.

There are many visionary and forward-looking cultures that have been developed in literature and other mediums. I have selected the Star Trek example because of its years of tenure and development by many creative people, including Gene Roddenberry, its original creator. Film and television can be very much like a microcosm of life, containing many if not mostly elements that a villager Community does. Through the course of creating many iterations and multiplicity of episodes, the Star Trek writers have envisioned and worked through countless problems, social and individual conflicts, growth points, and resolution scenarios.

While the Star Trek universe might seem like a distant and unrealistic ideal, it offers valuable insights into how we might reshape our economies and societies. There is a principle in success technologies that underscores our potential: what we can conceive, we can achieve. Star Trek certainly aids us in conceiving this future more clearly. The task may indeed seem daunting, but it is not only possible, it is set to be rewarding and even fun on many levels. Through visionary thinking, concerted effort, and the right policies, we can move closer to a world that values cooperation, diversity, sustainability, and the well-being of all its inhabitants.

Just as Indigenous Cultures have allowed us to understand previous localized communities in harmony with nature and one another, the Star Trek principles take us into the realm of futuristic ideals that align with this vision. While it may seem at first that living in space is very disconnected from living in a natural environment, living within a contained space, such as a ship, even a large one, requires an enormous circular economy, resource management, ecological practices, and conscientious social and personal behavior.

Seven Key Principles from the Star Trek Economic Model

The Star Trek universe offers us more than captivating narratives of space exploration; it provides a blueprint for a society where wealth isn't dictated by material accumulation but by the richness of personal development, societal contribution, and the common good. This futuristic, post-scarcity economy portrayed in the series, particularly within the United Federation of Planets (UFP), envisions a world that's starkly different from our current reality, yet profoundly inspiring.

While the UFP is a far cry from our present society, the principles that it is built upon serve as valuable guidance as we navigate the complex challenges of our time. These principles present a compelling alternative to our existing systems, challenging us to reevaluate our notions of wealth, success, and societal organization. However, implementing these principles is not as simple as replicating the Star Trek economy. It requires a thorough understanding and contextual adaptation to our existing societal, cultural, and economic norms.

In light of this, we have identified seven key principles from the Star Trek economy that, when interpreted and applied thoughtfully, can serve as stepping stones towards a more equitable and sustainable society. As an initial step, let's simply imagine how they might be able to be integrated into our current systems.

1. **Fostering a Culture of Cooperation:** A fundamental characteristic of the UFP model is its emphasis on cooperation over competition. Adapting this principle to our societies would involve shifting our business models towards more cooperative and collaborative structures. Policies encouraging partnerships and alliances between businesses, particularly in solving shared societal challenges, would help promote a culture of cooperation.

    Examples — Ways We Can Engender Cooperation over Competition

    Employee-Owned Businesses: Encourage the development of businesses where employees are shareholders. This can be done through legislative support and economic incentives that favor this business model. An example is the Mondragon Corporation in Spain, one of the largest cooperative corporations globally.

Cooperative Alliances: Companies can form cooperative alliances to collectively address global challenges, such as climate change or equitable distribution of resources. A successful case in point is the Fair Trade movement that unites producers, traders, and consumers in support of fair pricing and sustainable practices.

Shared Economy: Foster a "sharing economy" that promotes the use of shared resources, thereby reducing waste and promoting sustainability. Examples include car-sharing platforms like Zipcar and shared workspace businesses like WeWork.

2. **Redefining Wealth and Success:** We must move beyond the narrow definition of wealth as mere accumulation of material possessions. Instead, we can develop measures that value personal development, societal contributions, and the well-being of communities. Policies that prioritize these aspects of wealth, such as the development of alternative indicators to GDP, can be key in this shift.

    Examples: Ways We Can Redefine Wealth and Success

    Holistic Metrics: Adopt alternative measures to GDP that encompass a more comprehensive view of a nation's well-being, such as the Human Development Index (HDI) or the Social Progress Index (SPI).

Incentives for Social Contributions: Introduce incentives for corporations that prioritize social good over profits, such as tax benefits for social enterprises and businesses with strong corporate social responsibility (CSR) initiatives.

Value Non-Monetary Contributions: Recognize and value non-monetary contributions to society, such as volunteering and caregiving. For instance, countries like France include the value of household and care work in their national accounting systems.

3. **Ensuring Universal Basic Needs:** Inspired by the UFP's post-scarcity society, we should aspire to ensure that everyone has access to basic necessities such as food, shelter, healthcare, and education. This could be achieved through robust social safety nets, policies ensuring a living wage, and programs like universal basic income.

Examples: Ways We Can Ensure Universal Basic Needs Fulfillment

Universal Basic Income: Implement a universal basic income (UBI) scheme that provides all citizens with a certain amount of money, regardless of their employment status. Successful pilot projects in places like Finland and Kenya have demonstrated the potential of UBI in improving financial security and well-being.

While the vision of UBI improving lives is admirable, analysis of pilot studies reveals challenges. For instance, when Finland implemented a UBI trial for unemployed citizens from 2017-

2018, it led to minor improvements in well-being but no long-term boost in employment. This indicates that UBI alone may be insufficient. A balanced approach may be gradually expanding social welfare programs shown to enhance education and job opportunities, coupled with guaranteed income supplements for the unemployed or underemployed based on their specific needs.

Strong Social Safety Nets: Strengthen social safety nets by providing accessible and quality public healthcare, affordable housing, and free education. The Nordic countries like Denmark and Sweden have been successful models of this approach.

Food Security Programs: Establish food security programs that ensure access to nutritious food for all, such as subsidized community agriculture projects and farmer's markets in underserved areas.

4. **Valuing Diversity and Plurality:** The UFP model recognizes the value of diverse cultures and perspectives. In a practical sense, this implies creating inclusive economic systems that cater to different community needs and conditions. Policies promoting inclusivity and diversity in decision-making processes, as well as support for localized and Indigenous economic systems, can be steps in this direction.

Examples: Ways We Can Embrace Diversity and Plurality Cultural Preservation and Celebration: Encourage cultural preservation and celebration through education and events that honor different cultures. This helps to build understanding and appreciation of diversity.

Inclusive Policies and Legislation: Implement inclusive policies and legislation that safeguard against discrimination and promote diversity in all sectors of society, from education to employment.

Diverse Representation: Promote diverse representation in all forms of media, politics, and business leadership to ensure a broad range of perspectives are heard and considered.

5. **Promoting Sustainable Technologies**: While we do not yet possess the advanced technologies of the Star Trek universe, we have made significant strides in areas such as renewable energy, AI, and sustainable agriculture. Policies incentivizing the development and adoption of these technologies can help us transition toward a more sustainable economy.

Examples: Ways We Can Use Sustainable Technology for the Benefit of All

Accessible and Affordable Tech: Develop policies and initiatives that make technology accessible and affordable for everyone, thereby bridging the digital divide.

Open Source Movements: Support open source movements that allow for the free use, distribution, and modification of software and technology, thereby democratizing access to technology.

Tech for Social Good: Encourage the use of technology for social good, such as apps that promote sustainability, digital platforms for civic engagement, and AI that helps solve complex social issues.

6. **Environmental Stewardship:** Star Trek demonstrates a profound respect for all life forms and their habitats. We can learn to do the same, prioritizing environmental stewardship in our economic and political decisions.

    Examples: Ways We Can Encourage Environmental Stewardship

    Green Policies and Legislation: Implement policies and legislation that promote environmental sustainability, such as regulations limiting carbon emissions, incentives for renewable energy use, and penalties for environmental pollution.

    Sustainable Business Practices: Encourage businesses to adopt sustainable practices through incentives and certification programs, such as LEED certification for green building or B Corporation certification for overall sustainability.

    Public Education and Awareness: Promote public education and awareness about environmental issues and sustainable practices through school curricula, media campaigns, and community programs.

7. **Encouraging Lifelong Learning**

    In the UFP, individuals are free to pursue their passions and contribute to society through their interests and abilities. They are learners for life, constantly seeking knowledge and personal growth. We can encourage a similar culture of lifelong learning in our society.

Examples: Ways We Can Encourage Lifelong Learning

Support for Adult Education: Establish policies and funding mechanisms that support adult education programs. This could involve subsidies or tax credits for individuals pursuing further education or vocational training. Countries like Sweden and Canada have robust adult education programs that could serve as models.

Promote Online Learning Platforms: Encourage the use of online learning platforms that allow individuals to learn at their own pace. These platforms could offer a wide range of courses, from academic subjects to practical skills. Coursera, edX, and Khan Academy are examples of this approach.

Vocational Training Programs: Develop and promote vocational training programs that provide individuals with practical skills relevant to the job market. Germany's dual vocational training system, which combines classroom studies with on-the-job training, is a successful example of this strategy.

Incentivize Businesses to Provide Learning Opportunities: Encourage businesses to provide their employees with opportunities for further learning and skill development. This could be through on-site training programs, or by providing allowances for employees to pursue external courses or qualifications.

Community Learning Initiatives: Support community learning initiatives such as local workshops, public lectures, and skill-sharing meetups. These not only provide opportunities for learning but also foster community ties and promote a culture of shared knowledge.

By promoting a culture of lifelong learning, we can empower individuals to continually develop their skills, adapt to changing circumstances, and contribute to their communities in meaningful ways.

Let's seek to transcend these types of limitations and, to borrow a phrase, boldly go where no man has gone before, as we set our sights on a future full of promise and opportunity. With these forward-looking models as inspiration, we now circle back to the core tenets vital for an awakened crew of Spaceship Earth, integrating future ideals with ancient wisdom.

III.
THE VILLAGE MODEL

As we turn from the expansive lens of varied Indigenous cultures to more recent community structure, the core principles distilled from Indigenous wisdom remained our guiding lights in villages over the past millennia. One cannot help but marvel at the intricate fabric of community life weaved within many villages that sustained themselves for hundreds or thousands of years, as well as the practices that defined them.

As modern society ventures deeper into the technological age and individualistic expressions, there is a growing yearning to reestablish and experience the balance and harmony that villages once provided. Indeed, the concept of the village, while ancient, has remained the dominant social structure that nurtured humanity up to and into the modern age. Villages offer a timeless blueprint for holistic well-being that we would be wise to re-examine and integrate into the fabric of our communities.

In an essay called Utopia, Inc., Alexa Clay claims that humans are genetically programmed for tribal living, shaped by thousands of years of living in small bands, tribes, or villages; our evolution best suits us to live in small, tight-knit communities where cooperation and interdependence are necessary for survival. In modern times, we may have lost some of these connections due to factors such as urbanization and technology, but our DNA still reflects this tribal heritage and we still have an urge to be part of a modern village or tribal unit.

At their core, traditional villages embodied principles of collective governance, localized economies, skill preservation, and interdependent living that forged strong social bonds and resilience. Understanding and thoughtfully replicating these tenets can help ground our modern communities and pave the way for greater harmony.

Fundamental Village Principles

Collective Decision Making: Historically, villages operate on a consensus-driven model. Decisions were rarely made in isolation. Community assemblies, or gatherings of elders and representatives, ensure that a wide range of voices are heard. These consultations are rooted in the belief that every individual, irrespective of age or status, holds a unique piece of wisdom. Pooling this collective wisdom ensures that choices are well-rounded and equitable and upholds the village's broader well-being.

Resource Management: Communities can very effectively manage local resources, ensuring they meet their needs without depleting the resources. Who knows better the idiosyncrasies of local production, supply, and needs than the people who manage and depend upon them?

Circular Economy: Having a largely localized economic system allows for easy exchange of resources to be circulated through the village system. Products and materials are reused, repaired, or recycled instead of being thrown away after use. Keeping materials in use for as long as possible minimizes waste and maximizes the use of resources to reduce the environmental impact of production and consumption. It fosters community skills and creates a regenerative system that benefits both the environment and the economy.

Community Cohesion: The importance of togetherness is ingrained in every village activity. From daily chores like preparing meals to special occasions like weddings or harvest festivals, moments of collective participation are plenty. These regular interactions are more than mere traditions. They fortify community bonds, reinforce shared values, and lessen the feeling that members feel alone or isolated.

Microcosmic Self-Sufficiency: Ancient communities were often self-sufficient units, mastering a range of skills required to sustain themselves. Localizing production, supply, and consumption creates diversity and variety in the world, and self-sufficiency that ensures stability and resilience within the world society in the event of national or global supply-side failure.

Cyclical Living: Echoing our earlier exploration of cyclical time, village life encourages local food growth, harvesting, and seasonal activities, helping attune the community to the rhythms of nature. From sowing to harvesting, birth to death, celebrations to mourning, every phase can be acknowledged and revered in a tight interwoven village, teaching individuals the value of each other, timing, resilience, and gratitude.

Rekindling Communal Bonds: Communities organize festivities, rituals, and ceremonies in tandem with natural cycles, reinvigorating a shared bond not just among themselves but with nature too.

Sustainable Urban Planning: Cityscapes can integrate green spaces that align with seasonal changes, fostering an environment where residents can connect with nature's cycles despite urban settings.

Seasonal Festivals: Re-embracing traditional festivals aligned with solar and lunar cycles can help communities come together in celebration of nature's rhythms. Whether it's the solstice, equinox, or harvest festivals, these gatherings can serve as communal reminders of our intricate bond with the environment.

Renewable Energy Push: Harnessing energy from cyclical sources like the sun and wind aligns our modern energy needs with nature's rhythms. Solar panels and wind turbines are a nod to respecting and utilizing the Earth's natural and recurring energy cycles, rather than depleting finite resources.

Personal and Community Gardening: In an era dominated by fast food and instant gratification, taking the time to plant, nurture, and harvest one's own food is a profound reconnection to the cycles of nature. Whether it's a sprawling backyard garden, community allotments, or simple container gardens on a balcony, the act of growing food is therapeutic and enlightening. It fosters a deep appreciation for the processes of life, from germination to fruition.

Even in densely populated urban centers like Manhattan, where space is a premium, innovative solutions like sprout gardens can thrive. These require minimal space, can be set up on windowsills or countertops, and provide a constant supply of fresh, nutritious greens.

Grown Locally Movement: Embracing the ethos of "Farm to Table," the Grown Locally movement reconnects people to the land and helps encourage food production close to home. Consumers are becoming more conscious of seasonal produce, aligning their diets with what the earth yields naturally in their geographic vicinity at different times of the year. Not only does this ensure fresher, more nutritious meals, but it also promotes a cyclical understanding of agriculture and reduces the carbon footprint associated with transporting non-local goods.

Urban Green Spaces: Beyond the integration of parks and forests, cities can be designed with green rooftops, vertical gardens, and communal vegetable patches that change with the seasons. Such initiatives not only provide residents with a touch of nature but also serve as a constant reminder of the cyclical nature of life.

Modern Tribal Movements

There are many subcultures and communities that could be considered "modern tribal models" due to their shared values, practices, or experiences. Here are a few:

> **The LGBT Movement:** One such modern tribe is the LGBT community. Despite vast geographic distances, varied socio-economic backgrounds, and age differences, many within the

LGBT community experience a profound sense of tribal connection. Their shared experiences of understanding identity, confronting societal norms, and advocating for rights have fostered a global community that is bonded by more than just shared sexual or gender identities. This tribe epitomizes the power of shared experiences in shaping communal bonds that transcend traditional societal divisions.

Festival Culture: Music and arts festivals, especially transformational festivals like Burning Man, Boom, or Rainbow Gathering, foster a unique tribal culture. Attendees often share values of self-expression, community, artistry, and spirituality. These festivals often have their own set of norms and principles that foster a sense of belonging and identity.

Ayahuasca and Plant Medicines Culture: The resurgence of interest in traditional plant medicines like ayahuasca, peyote, and psilocybin mushrooms has given rise to communities centered around ceremonial and therapeutic use. These groups often value spiritual growth, emotional healing, and a deep respect for Indigenous traditions.

Permaculture and Ecovillage Movements: Individuals and groups dedicated to sustainable living and holistic land management practices often form tight-knit communities, like the Findhorn Foundation in Scotland or Auroville in India. They value sustainability, community living, and harmony with nature.

Urban Farming Communities: In many cities, communities are forming around the concept of urban farming and gardening. These tribes value self-sufficiency, local food, and community resilience.

Tiny House and Van Life Movements: People who prioritize minimalist living and mobility have formed a unique community. They share tips, gather at conventions, and foster a culture of simplicity and sustainability.

Meditation and Mindfulness Communities: Groups that center around practices like Vipassana, Zen, or transcendental meditation form tribes focused on inner peace, spiritual exploration, and mindfulness.

Extreme Sports Communities: Be it rock climbing, paragliding, or parkour, enthusiasts of these sports form tight-knit groups with shared adrenaline-pumping experiences and values of pushing physical and mental boundaries.

Alternative Education Movements: Homeschooling, unschooling, or forest schooling communities come together over shared educational philosophies and practices, offering support and resources to each other.

These modern tribal models offer individuals a sense of belonging and purpose, often providing a counter-narrative to mainstream culture. They can be seen as reactions to a rapidly changing world, with individuals seeking deeper connections, meaning, and more aligned ways of living.

Cultivating Community Knowledge and Skills

The traditional village is a living university. Skills aren't just learned; they are directly passed on and ingrained through hands-on experiences. Craftsmanship, farming techniques, storytelling, healing practices, and many other talents.

Generations of Skills in Community: Community mentorship goes well beyond teaching vocational skills. Experienced elders mentor the younger generation, ensuring the perpetuation of wisdom, culture, emotional intelligence, and traditions. In a well-rounded and diverse village or community, knowledge is valued and passed down through generations. Master-apprentice relationships are cherished, ensuring not only the survival of these skills but also their evolution of character, refined through each subsequent generation. From pottery to weaving, herbal medicine to construction, practical skills, stories, and values are nurtured in a cohesive social system, a dynamic that naturally acknowledges the contributions of individual members and also expands the community's overall stability and resilience.

Oral Traditions: Myths, legends, and histories were shared orally on a direct personal level, embedding cultural wisdom in memorable narratives and elevating the importance of local community members rather than global social media influencers or bloggers.

Shared Parenting: The saying "It takes a village to raise a child" is deeply rooted in communal living. In the village setup, child-rearing isn't solely the parents' responsibility. Aunts, uncles, neighbors, elders — everyone plays a part. This distributed parenting system ensures that children are exposed to a wealth of knowledge, values, and skill sets. Moreover, it cultivated a deep-seated feeling of belonging and security, knowing that the entire community had their back.

Educational Integration: Schools can incorporate curricula that blend cyclical wisdom with linear progress, offering students a holistic understanding of growth and development.

Art and Cultural Expressions Reflecting Cyclical Time: Modern artists, musicians, and writers can create works that celebrate and highlight the cyclical patterns of life, making the understanding of cyclical time more accessible and relatable to younger generations.

Blue Zones Practices: Blue Zones researchers have identified several common lifestyle practices that contribute to the remarkable health and longevity observed in these communities. These include:

1. Plant-based diets: Blue Zone residents consume a largely plant-based diet, with a focus on whole foods, legumes, and nuts.

2. Regular physical activity: Movement is naturally integrated into daily life through activities like gardening, walking, and manual labor.

3. Strong social connections: Close-knit communities and a sense of belonging are prioritized, with regular social interaction and engagement.

4. Purpose and spirituality: Having a clear sense of purpose, often rooted in spiritual or religious beliefs, is common among Blue Zone residents.

5. Stress reduction: Techniques like meditation, napping, and spending time in nature help manage stress and promote relaxation.

The Blue Zones platform offers powerful examples of how aligning our lifestyles with principles of balance, simplicity, and connection to nature and community can yield remarkable benefits for our health and well-being, while also promoting the health of the planet. As we navigate the challenges ahead, we can draw inspiration and guidance from these models, adapting their wisdom to our modern context to create a more sustainable, harmonious way of life. By integrating these practices into our own communities, we can cultivate the knowledge and skills necessary to build resilience, foster well-being for generations to come, and contribute to the healing of our Earth.

As we navigate the complexities of modern life, integrating the timeless social innovations of villages can help ground our communities in values of collaboration, sustainability, and mutual support. Blending ancestral wisdom with modern technology and design thinking, models like eco-villages, agrihoods[2] and the Blue Zone projects are reimagining human settlements to foster collective thriving.

Though the modern context differs, the traditional village still has much to teach us. Its principles illuminate pathways to resilient, socially enriching, and ecologically wise communities where solutions

---

2 Agrihoods are residential communities that are built around a working farm or agricultural space, with the goal of promoting sustainable living, community engagement, and access to fresh produce.

are woven, not imposed. By rediscovering and reinterpreting village wisdom, we can build human-scale settlements where generations are nurtured and lives lived in greater harmony with each other and with nature.

The resurgence of such practices in modern society doesn't just offer a way to sustainably feed ourselves. It represents a broader return to understanding and embracing cyclical time and living in harmony with nature. Every seed sown and sprout harvested is a step towards recognizing the continuous cycles that govern our existence and a celebration of our deep-rooted connection to nature.

In weaving these examples into the fabric of modernity, societies can build a bridge between the linear progression that dominates today and the cyclical wisdom of yesteryears. In doing so, a balance is struck, promoting a more sustainable, harmonious, and interconnected future.

In this expanded perspective, our connection to the Earth is deepened. We see clearly that our planet is not just our home, but the life-supporting system on which we rely. This galactic view does not replace our cyclical or linear perspectives, but rather integrates with them, offering a more holistic understanding of our place in the cosmos.

Our responsibility then becomes twofold: to deeply nurture our planet, the very soil that supports and sustains us, and simultaneously to expand our consciousness, reaching for the stars, maybe one day becoming a galactic community. It's a hybrid model, requiring a delicate balance between rooting deeply into our biological source of life, while not limiting our growth and exploration or our part in the cosmic blueprint.

Indeed, the deeper our understanding and the higher our aspirations, the greater the need for strong roots. Just as a tall tree requires a deep root system to stand firmly and reach high, so too must we, as a species, anchor ourselves in the Indigenous wisdom of our roots and the expanded view of our planet, as we reach for the integrated possibilities of our future. We embrace both the soil and the stars, as the crew and the passengers on this journey through time and space.

Envisioning the Future: From Consumption to Evolution

In this age of information, we are witnessing a shift in the paradigm of how societies plan and implement change. The days of top-down, bureaucratic planning are fading into the background as we usher in an era of collective decision-making and participatory evolution. Thanks to advancements in technologies such as artificial intelligence, it is now possible to create dynamic, adaptive models that reflect the collective wisdom of humanity.

We have never had so much information available to help us be able to plan our course, from evaluating the good qualities of past societies to envisioning the future, to planning the logistics of the present; we have the tools available to make the shifts we need, we must also have the desire and clarity to see beyond our limitations and distractions and make the transitions.

Our choices reveal our character. Will we be able to redefine 'progress' towards balance with true justice and compassion? Or remain chained by unhealthy drives and systems, unable to see past our short-term self-interest? The time to break free of internal and external restraints is now. Together, we can create a future guided not by irrational appetites or control by the fortunate few, but by our highest ideals. We will need to break free of external as well as internal restraint systems to become liberated to make the right decisions and act upon them.

Part 2
Charting a New Course

Why do we never get an answer when we're knocking at the door
With a thousand million questions about hate and death and war?
'Cause when we stop and look around us, there is nothing that we need
In a world of persecution that is burning in its greed

Justin Hayward
Moody Blues

IV.
Breaking Free of Unhealthy Restraints

"Veni, vidi, vici." This famous Latin phrase, translated as "I came, I saw, I conquered," is a reflection of a bygone era where conquest and domination were seen as commendable traits. This can mirror a mindset often found among more than just those who have accumulated excessive wealth: "I am not a loser, I am a winner. Why not more? Money is a way of keeping score, and I want to win bigger." Distinguishing ourselves from the masses, and standing out from the pack attracts notoriety, yet, embracing the liberation of loss can be quite illuminating.

In the early eighties, I was presented an award by my company where they announced to me that I was now in the top 1% of income earners in America and that I had reached the Pinnacle of success. I was the Man. I was the King of the Mountain. After I was on the podium another top producer in the company came up to me and shared that now that I was on top, the pressure now was to be able to stay there. For whatever reason his words resonated within me as a realization that if this is the grand prize, something was wrong, something was really missing.

In the King of the Hill, the champions all compete to reach the top of the mountain from every direction. The base of the mountain is so great that at first, they can only see their own path upward, the top so high that it is hidden above the clouds. Many climbers are trampled underfoot by the fittest racers along the way. Finally, some break above the clouds of Mount Olympus, the peak of economic competition. However, when I saw beyond the clouds, I looked out and thought to myself in horror, "This is no mountain, this is a giant mound made up entirely of the discarded bodies of the previous waves of champions, trampled and buried under the onslaught of the never-ending waves that follow. There is no direction to go but up because we cannot turn back through the impenetrable wall of new competitors. "

I chose to be buried hoping to find a reincarnation in a new life. This is a sad realization, but it is how I see today's trophy of success. In our economic system, there is no award for most of us who strive to contribute their real value. There is only more money for "winners," on a mountaintop of emptiness where the best of the best shut off their feelings while being able to take the most at the expense of others. It is a guilty victory often masked by the need to go for more, hoping there is yet a higher peak where it fulfills their needs. There is not. It is simply the wrong direction.

I now proudly consider myself a "loser," a label I wear with a sense of liberation. Over time, I've cultivated a genuine affection for letting go of all kinds of things or ideas I once valued as integral parts of my self-image of being successful. My college speech coach, Shawn, illustrated this vividly in a parable. The story involves capturing monkeys using a coconut with a hole just wide enough for a monkey's hand. Attached to a tree and filled with candy, the coconut becomes an irresistible but cunning trap. The monkey reaches in to grasp the candy but finds itself ensnared, unable to withdraw its hand while clinging to the sugary prize. The creature's overwhelming desire for something so fleeting leads it into captivity, typically ending in a zoo — the ultimate domestic prison.

This poignant story serves as a metaphor for my own life revelations. Many of the things I've clung to are akin to the "candy in the coconut," luring me into a trap fueled by misguided desires and a misunderstanding of the game at hand. While it is obvious that a huge bank account provides the opportunity to buy whatever we want and gives us a sense of freedom, larger estates also require more effort to maintain and hold onto. Maybe, then we have to hire a maid, a gardener, and a chef to feed them? When I was in the top-earner lifestyle, I did not like that it cast me into a rarefied stratosphere, where it was hard for me to know who to trust when it seemed like everyone wanted something from me.

Upon introspection, I've realized that letting go — whether it's of excess weight, cumbersome obligations, or limiting beliefs — often provides a greater sense of freedom than accumulating ever can. I have had the opportunity to spend time with some prominent celebrities and they often are surrounded by a support system of keepers who need to keep the goose that lays golden eggs protected so they can ensure their lucrative enterprise continues producing. A friend of mine from a prominent family shared with me that If a man is put in iron shackles, he will fight to be a slave. But if cast in gold, he will willingly put them on and wear them proudly as a trophy of success.

As we chart a course towards a future that holds the promise of harmony, equity, and sustainability, it becomes crucial to see and understand the deep-rooted restraints and invisible chains, often disguised as societal norms or fueled by unchecked power dynamics, that bind our thoughts and actions. These restraints deter us from realizing our full potential and prevent society from acting in its best collective interest. To harness the transformative potential of innovative models and share plans that express the power of our collective intentions, we must muster the courage to break free.

The journey we're embarking on now is not just an outward fixing of problems, it is also a deep inward realigning of what we value, how we see ourselves, and our life path. We have millennia of conditioning encrusted over our unencumbered vision that had its value in its day but is now obsolete. We have other layers of conditioning that are being newly laid upon us as control mechanisms of sovereigns, governments, and institutions of power.

An example of controlling collective belief might be the stigma and negative spin put on those who wrn of the COVID-19 Mrna effects and are labeled "conspiracy theorists." This stigma strategically dissuades people from sharing and discussing what they observe in the world around them, from policies of dysfunctional leadership to pandemics, social branding, economic restraints, and ecological policies. A recent example would be the much larger number of top-level fit young athletes, such as Bronny James, LeBron James' eldest son and one of the most well-known college athletes, who suffered sudden cardiac arrest. Another example was on January 2, 2023, during a Monday Night Football game between the Buffalo Bills and the Cincinnati Bengals. Buffalo Bills safety Damar Hamlin collapsed on the field after suffering a cardiac arrest. Any public figure who even mentioned the possibility that this was a vaccine side effect has been subsequently and publicly viciously attacked, even though statistics reveal that the occurrence of this event is up over 1500% since the COVID-19 Mrna Vaccine, far beyond a mere statistical anomaly.

To better understand this dynamic, we will briefly reflect upon the historical evolution of human societies to look at layers of historical conditioning. Each stage of societal development has been marked by distinct economic and political systems that have shaped how we see the world, how resources are distributed, how social order is maintained, and how relationships are formed and managed. From simple nomadic collectives, through the systemic exploitation embedded in slave societies to the socio-economic hierarchies of feudalism, our ancestors collectively lived through distinct models for organizing societies that remain deeply embedded in our psyches.

Starting with the nomadic hunter-gatherer societies, human civilizations have traversed stages of primitive communism, where resources were shared collectively, and there was little concept of private ownership. Our DNA reflects this evolutionary history, and we still crave the sense of belonging and connection that comes from being part of a tribe. These tribal bands engaged strong social connections, shared resources, and created a sense of belonging to a community. The stakes were high and the challenges substantial. Each individual was required to play a vital role that directly supported the communal unit's ability to survive and flourish.

Tribal nomadic bands gave way to variations of early empires and collectives. Humans experienced many variations from absolutist monarchies that wielded unchecked power that resided in the hands of dictatorships and absolute control of a single leader or group, to fiefdoms where the private ownership emphasized in early capitalism. These many economic and political systems have marked significant epochs in our societal development.

The advent of socialism and communism introduced concepts of state or community-owned means of production and aimed at equal distribution of wealth. However, these systems had their pitfalls and often resulted in authoritarian regimes where dictators or small groups came into similar power in a different direction.

One trend is apparent. Many people believe that the power of the people is in the hands of a few very powerful and wealthy individuals who put their needs ahead of the majority. Many stories, television, and movie plots place powerful and wealthy members of society on the seat of an existing oligarchy. These powerful people run the world and have strategically funded and set up dictatorships and sabotaged socialist government structures to demonstrate that they do not work. Of course, this theory would qualify as a conspiracy theory, and almost anyone with influence, wealth, or power can deny such conspiracies on any large scale of public control by those in power.

I have met some quite wealthy and powerful people and politicians and spent time with certain major celebrities. What I have never encountered is any powerful individual who appears to be able to control their destiny and does not have to answer to someone on top of them. It is like the power structure in this world is taller than Mount Everest, and the peak is on the other side of impenetrable clouds. Does anyone know who's actually in charge here? It is certainly not the president or other high-level politicians in America.

In the late 1990s, I was part of a creative team that worked on turning Robert Anton Wilson's Illuminatus trilogy into a movie series. In the series, he describes Leviathan as a sort of psychic internet that controls a vast amount of information and influences the minds of individuals. Leviathan is a metaphorical representation of a vast, decentralized network of communication and information exchange that exists within the human psyche. It is described as being like a psychic internet that controls much of human behavior and society. Who is really in power? Humans, demons, extraterrestrials? Who knows, but whatever it is, it will be the ruin of us all, and it needs to be removed from control in favor of a rational, intelligent planning matrix by and for the people.

I'm not particularly fond of individuals solely relying on passive wealth, as it can divert their energy from making creative contributions and sometimes even lead to less constructive lifestyles. However, I firmly believe that affluent individuals who possess both the resources and the desire to create a positive impact can play a significant role in the transformation discussed in this book. I would welcome the opportunity to connect with more wealthy individuals who exhibit these positive qualities and are willing to actively engage in addressing the critical issues crucial to our transformation.

While we see aspects of socialistic systems combined in various forms in many societies today, the adoption of the more successful elements of this system has not been swift or straightforward. It often has been vehemently opposed in capitalist countries, such as the United States of America. Different societies have experienced these dynamics in varying degrees of intensity and form. Acknowledging this complex and layered history is crucial as we look to break free from these unhealthy patterns and shift towards a future where equity, sustainability, and interconnectedness become the norm, not the exception.

Among these evolutionary influencers, one formidable system has risen to prominence — ***capitalism***. Its reach pervades every facet of our modern world and lives, sculpting the socioeconomic landscape that defines our global community. However, in its current form, capitalism has aspects that have become a double-edged sword, both fueling our progress and exacerbating societal and ecological imbalances.

Within America, there is often a very strong belief system ingrained into our cultural perspective that capitalism, unbridled, is the best means of deriving solutions and that any form of socialistic governmental system is less effective than a *free market economy*.

To address this belief, I would point out that statistical evidence reveals America is only ranked about 75th in the world in citizen satisfaction. Almost every country in the world that is rated in the top 50 by its citizens for overall quality of life and satisfaction contains significant elements of some socialized structure. The number of people falling between the cracks in America, the homeless, the incarcerated, the high ratio of police forces, those unable to get proper medical treatment, or the young who cannot afford a higher education — all this is staggeringly off. These people represent an enormously undervalued and underutilized portion of society, which instead of being rehabilitated or empowered to become productive contributors to their communities, are simply discarded or even trampled.

At least in America, the country has evolved a form of housing for millions of the displaced. These mobile dwellings are now among the most prevalent forms of affordable housing in use, with millions of units in operation. They clearly demonstrate just how willing the country is to adequately address the needs of the less fortunate portion of its society.

ACTIVATING THE CREW OF SPACESHIP EARTH

In this section, we will explore aspects of capitalism that have become the current dominant block to our societal transformation. We will examine its attributes and its ailments, seeking to understand its powerful grip on our collective psyche and its role in the widening wealth and resource gap. In the following section, I will share aspects of my realization and analogy of how aspects of unhealthy capitalism parallel the physiologic dynamics of cancer and its specific processes of growth and dominance over a body under its control.

This will not be a one-sided critique; we will also look at the historical benefits and the potential of capitalism. Like all systems, it is a tool that can be wielded for harm or for good. We will explore the reforms and alternatives that could redirect capitalism's immense energy toward balanced and sustainable growth.

While capitalism has undoubtedly driven innovation and economic growth in many respects, we must acknowledge these benefits with nuance. Capitalism is neither an intrinsic good nor an intrinsic evil. Rather, it is a multifaceted economic system that, much like technology, can be channeled towards life-affirming or destructive ends based on how it is wielded.

The positive impacts do not negate the other critiques of capitalism's harm. They do provide a perspective for why, with thoughtful reforms, capitalism can potentially be steered in a more equitable and sustainable direction aligned with human welfare. Unchecked capitalism consumes all in its path. There must be proper safeguards and oversight to nurture balanced growth and meaningful contributions to the collective rather than unequal excess to the few.

Our aim is not to take an extremist stance for or against capitalism as a whole but to honestly assess its light and shadows, risks and potentials. Capitalism, like technology, should be guided by ethical considerations, not merely profit motives.

Larry Fink, the billionaire chief of BlackRock, which manages upwards of $9 trillion in assets, has been attacked by certain Wall Street concerns and spinners for being a promoter of socialism and undermining the American way of the free market. In his annual letters to CEOs, Fink has pushed companies to focus less on short-term profits and quarterly earnings, and more on their long-term social purpose. He has urged corporate leaders to invest in their workers, reduce their environmental footprint, and positively contribute to society.

Fink has backed up his rhetoric with action at BlackRock. He has committed to sustainability measures like divesting from fossil fuels, pressured companies that BlackRock invests in to disclose their environmental risks, and launched funds that screen out environmentally damaging companies.

However, Fink has become a lightning rod for criticism from conservatives due to his push for environmental, social, and corporate governance (ESG) investing over the past few years. Critics argue his brand of stakeholder capitalism undermines free markets and shareholder primacy. But Fink maintains that companies focused on their social impact and stakeholders will have greater long-term profitability compared to those obsessed with short-term gains. He believes business should serve society, not just maximize returns for investors. As head of the world's largest asset manager, he has pushed other companies and investors to adopt this socially conscious approach.

I believe Mr. Fink is right about his socially conscious approach to business. It makes sense that as the general public becomes more aware of these critical issues, those companies that have operated on a destructive level are likely to be ostracized by the purchasing public and sales will suffer accordingly.

I have personally known a handful of very wealthy individuals who had or have very developed character, perspective, and ethics. Albeit, they were the exception in my world. From what I observed, they have done tremendous good for those around them and society in general. Almost anyone I met who had any consistent contact with them thought the world of them. I wish these individuals were still alive today because I believe they would help fuel this transformation. I applaud those who are actually able to manage significant wealth, do good with it, and not be caught up in the self-serving ignorance that material consciousness with great affluence can produce. I hope that they recognize themselves as members of the crew of Spaceship Earth and are willing to play their part for the benefit of all, including themselves.

With wisdom and vigilance, capitalism's immense engine of innovation and productivity has and will be harnessed for shared prosperity. The future lies not in dismantling capitalism but in conscious redesign and further environmental, social, and corporate governance — with a significant emphasis on the environment.

In this spirit of nuance, we will continue exploring capitalism's benefits and its flaws that demand remedy, as well as reforms that can align it with ecological sustainability and social justice. Here are five key ways capitalism has benefited humanity:

1. **Driving technological innovation:** The profit motive in capitalism incentivizes investment in research, development, and bringing new inventions and technologies to market. This has accelerated innovation and brought advances in

healthcare, transportation, computing, communications, and more that improve quality of life.

2. **Increasing overall economic productivity:** Capitalist systems are associated with greater economic productivity by encouraging competition, efficiency, and access to capital. This expands the economic pie, increasing the goods and services available to society. Studies show capitalist economies have grown faster over the long run than more planned economic systems.

3. **Allocating resources effectively:** Prices and supply-demand dynamics in capitalist systems help allocate resources optimally towards the most valued ends. Capital flows to where it is most productive. This ensures a rational allocation of limited resources compared to more centrally planned approaches.

4. **Promoting individual economic freedom:** Capitalism enables individuals to have control over their economic decisions as owners of private property and the freedom to start businesses, invest capital, and pursue opportunities. This economic freedom allows people to improve their material well-being.

5. **Lifting many out of poverty:** Economic growth under capitalism has enabled rising material prosperity and lifted millions out of extreme poverty. Falling poverty rates worldwide correlate with the spread of capitalistic elements like international trade and private enterprise in developing

nations. Greater opportunity and higher standards of living have been achieved.

Of course, capitalism also has many flaws and downsides as the book discusses. Unchecked capitalism can lead to unsafe working conditions, environmental damage, concentrations of power, inequality, and more. But acknowledging some of its benefits provides a balanced perspective, rather than just vilifying the system outright. With judicious regulation and reform, capitalism can be harnessed for human progress while mitigating its downsides.

In breaking free from these unhealthy restraints, I am not proposing the wholesale abandonment of systems that have served us. Instead, I suggest a deep and comprehensive reassessment, a recalibration aimed at better aligning these systems with the principles of equity, sustainability, and interconnectedness. Our goal is not to dismantle, but to reshape and redirect, allowing us to fully embrace the potential of evolving models we can use to build the society we ideally would envision together.

The journey to understanding starts with diagnosing the problem. So, let's begin by peeling back the layers, examining the structure and dynamics of capitalism in its current state, and exploring potential solutions.

Diagnosing the Growing Problems with Capitalism

In our journey towards identifying the root causes of the current crises we face, we inevitably arrive at a critical examination of our prevailing economic system — *capitalism*. (At least the flavor of it that is commonly called "crony capitalism" vs. the classic "free market" version.) While it has undeniably driven significant technological and societal advancements, the unchecked growth of capitalism has also led to concerning disparities and destructive practices. I felt the analysis of the growing problems with capitalism was so important that it could be the sole focus of an entire book. However, I condensed it into parts in two chapters of this book because I realized that focusing on the problem without providing significant and tangible solutions would not accomplish my intention of encouraging new paths to remedy our collective dilemma and help us create a future in which we want to live.

Following the narrative thread of unchecked growth and the ensuing social and environmental ramifications, we must address the intricate stratagems and tactics employed by the oligarchy and the wealthiest individuals and corporations to maintain their grip on power and control. Over time, their strategies have become incredibly sophisticated, supported by massive banks of underground supercomputers that review all the world population's communications and activities, enforced by military and intelligence regimes, almost representing an updated, contemporary version of the classic literature model, the "Art of War."

Note: *The Art of War*, an ancient treatise penned by the Chinese military general and philosopher Sun Tzu between 475 and 221 B.C.E., is renowned for its timeless wisdom. Historically used as a guide to military strategy, it has permeated a variety of domains beyond the battlefield. Military strategists, political leaders, intelligence communities, and even players in the fields of business, politics, and sports have found value in its insights.

Now, it seems the principles of the *Art of War* have found a new application. The wealthiest and most powerful in society, perhaps consciously or unconsciously, appear to have co-opted some of Sun Tzu's strategies to maintain control and further their interests. However, rather than combating an external enemy, these tactics are turned inward, influencing the language and narrative of the socio-economic landscape and engaging the wider populace in battles of conflict and confusion, where the stakes are for the very fabric of our society and the health of our planet. While many people see and acknowledge the results of this dynamic, far fewer have clarified and understand the tool chest and methodology employed to execute it.

In our current age, marked by unprecedented levels of transparency and interconnectedness, a growing number of individuals both in America and worldwide are coming to a startling realization. They perceive a form of "organized crime" to be in the driver's seat of global affairs — an elite oligarchy that is more powerful than any nation, government, or form of normal checks and balances. It seems they control the very governments that we have created to protect the public interest. However, this viewpoint extends beyond the traditional concept of organized crime typified by mafia-like organizations. Instead, it encompasses a complex network of alliances and collaborations across a multitude of powerful entities fueled by the currency of "big money."

Intriguingly, these groups often appear unconnected or even diametrically opposed to one another, as exemplified by the seemingly antagonistic American two-party system. Thus, this intricate web of power conceals its allegiances, while it extends its reach. They subtly shape our world in ways that might not be immediately apparent and are intentionally hidden from view by powerful, organized intelligence agencies whose ranks are fortified with potent non-disclosure agreements that are enforced and punishable by prosecution for high treason for those who divulge their classified knowledge.

In the late 1990s, while writing a screenplay called *The Most Powerful Hand* about JFK's assassination, I discovered and dramatized how JFK, alongside his allies, such as Castro, and family members, attempted to prevent organized crime from taking control of the world. Since before JFK's assassination, a form of network, far removed from the stereotypical concept of the Italian Mafia, started to form and has evolved into a syndicate of power, operating at a level that influences the very fabric and direction of global society.

Knowing what I do, I am both surprised and see a glimmer of hope on the political scene that Robert F. Kennedy Jr. has entered the presidential race. It is interesting to me how media spinners, bought and paid for, undermine RFK, Jr., such as by calling him an anti-vaxxer. The media rarely acknowledges his true stance is against mercury in vaccines, not the vaccines themselves. His stance against mercury in vaccines is so obviously beneficial, yet the spin masters know that so few people can figure out the deeper truth, so their attacks will work to dissuade his support. They pass along inaccurate and biased arguments, supporting the stance of Big Pharma, even though the slant is not in the best interest of the public. I applaud Robert for his courage to try and break through these walls! If he somehow finds the support needed to win, he will likely be a game changer as President — or soon dead, like his father and uncle before him.

JFK failed in his mission, just as I failed to create the movie. I dropped it in 1998 after my life was threatened and my Hollywood production company obliterated, along with a very clear warning not to proceed. I should note that I had other controversial environmental programs that also attracted the negative attention of the border containers of Pleasantville.

It is my observation that this mafia-like consortium or new oligarchy, which I often refer to as the New Age Pharaohs, has established a complex nexus between many intelligence communities, major global corporations, financial institutions, the Federal Reserve, banking consortiums, multinational corporations, and oil money empires; that funnels its control structure down into societies through governments, intelligence agencies and components within the infrastructure of the modern world. These entities, whether through intent or circumstance, have shaped a system that can influence governments, dictate economic and social policies, and maintain control over significant aspects of our global society.

I openly acknowledge that this kind of concerted coordinated team effort could never be assembled without having a very compelling story that they are doing the right thing and that they are the good guys. I have read arguments on governmental oversight levels questioning, "Who do we want to manage the blackmarket's drug money? The CIA or illegal drug cartels?" On the surface, these seem like compelling arguments. So I checked an AI platform to get its opinion, and it came back with this — "Neither the CIA nor drug cartels should manage the black market's money. The black market is illegal and any involvement by government agencies or criminal organizations would only perpetuate illegal activities and harm society." I guess the same logic would hold true for human sex trafficking and pedophilia dealers.

I am not a proponent of disassembling a global governmental structure, such as the CIA's drug trade consortium, but I am a proponent of internal planning to be conducted with a very high state of reverence and a perspective that the mission is first and foremost to support the well-being of the human race, and to preserve the stability of the ecosystem. These agencies must also have a primary agenda to protect the health of the still-existing variety and beauty of nature on this exquisite and lovely planet. The Earth is not just primarily our bread basket to use and abuse at our sole discretion for personal or organizational gain.

We cannot allow agencies to disregard their responsibility to future generations, or help the multinational companies excavate and consume all of the resources of the earth as fast as we can excavate, hunt, or develop them. Concurrently, the majority of the population is kept preoccupied, their attention diverted by a relentless barrage of distractions or locked in an ever-increasing struggle for basic survival needs that enables the consortium to execute its agenda largely unchecked, thus perpetuating a cycle of control and exploitation.

The strategy is simple — distract the masses while we do what we want with the Earth.

Leadership By Unrestrained Greed or Guided Growth?

Capitalism, in essence, is an economic system that champions competition and the pursuit of self-interest. However, an essential question arises — where is the line between healthy competition and unrestrained greed? In a system where the wealthy have an ever-increasing advantage, dominance, and influence over the rest of the people, when does the pursuit of self-interest become detrimental to the collective good? Is making the rich richer really going to allow the majority to solve the ills and challenges our society is facing in a way that also supports the people of the world who care about the Earth and her health?

I recognized years ago how the Biblical story from Matthew 8:28-8:32 offers a contemplative reflection of dynamics today. The narrative speaks of demons in men who when they know Jesus will cast them out, they seek refuge in a herd of swine. When Jesus cast them into the swine, they run off a cliff and plunge to their doom in the sea below. I realized how this story might mirror today's dynamics where today's oligarchy, blinded by unbridled ambition and insatiable greed, is leading humanity towards a precipice and off a cliff of doom and destruction. This story stands as a clear warning for me to be discerning when compromised leaders offer guidance when they are actually acting in their own self-interest.

I want to acknowledge that there are many public servants who do their work for good reasons and with positive intentions. These individuals provide valuable services that benefit people. However, our governmental system has a top-down structure where those at lower levels must follow the directives handed down by superiors. As you go higher up in the hierarchy, the motivations and policies seem to become more distorted, rather than more transparent. The people making the decisions at the highest levels appear less focused on the common good and more influenced by obscure agendas. So while many public servants have good motives, the system itself corrupts the process and undermines serving the public interest.

Without much stronger regulatory checks and balances in place, capitalism's emphasis on unguided growth and profit maximization will lead to even greater exploitative practices and a disregard for social and environmental consequences. This kind of growth, reminiscent of a herd of possessed swine or a runaway train, is not sustainable or healthy for our societies or our planet. I find value in coining poignant phrases and I call this current dynamic "The March of The New World Pharaohs," which is part of "The Mad Race to Nowhere."

Wealth Accumulation and the Widening Resources Gap

Most people have played the board game Monopoly, and probably learned that once somebody has accumulated enough real estate and money, the other players have no chance of doing anything but going broke. Unless someone has a very unique gift, it is practically impossible to compete against a massive imbalance of accumulated wealth. I have had enterprises ripped out from under me by the wealthy and powerful.

The parallel within our current economic system is obvious. The stark, ever-growing disparity makes competing in the so-called "free-market" system completely out of balance and stacked against anyone who has less than millions of dollars to work with. The "free market" system is anything but free. Remember the twisted Golden Rule: *He who has the gold makes the rules.* This power imbalance has become the very hallmark of capitalism. The reign is fixed and the March of the New World Pharaohs is well underway.

The stark and growing inequality of wealth and resources in America is evident when examining the data. According to a 2020 study by Carter C. Price and Kathryn Edwards of the RAND Corporation, income inequality has exploded since 1975, with the top 1% capturing almost all economic gains. They calculate that had more equitable income distributions from 1945-1974 persisted, the aggregate annual income of Americans in the bottom 90% would have been $2.5 trillion higher in 2018. This equates to an astonishing amount of over $50 trillion redistributed from the bottom 90% to the top over the past four decades.

From 1947-1974, real incomes grew uniformly across all income levels, fostering a thriving middle class. However, around 1975 this era ended, as the top 1% rapidly pulled away from the rest of Americans. For example, a typical person earning $35,000 today would have earned $26,000 more if inequality had simply held constant. This extreme concentration of wealth has made America less resilient in crises like the COVID-19 pandemic.

The data substantiates that unrestrained capitalism since the 1970s has dramatically exacerbated inequality, with the gains of growth almost exclusively flowing to those at the very top at the expense of the broad population. This wealth concentration is not just anecdotal, but a systemic result of capitalism's current form.

According to economists Emmanuel Saez and Gabriel Zucman, the wealth gap has exploded due to tax policies favoring the rich, such as the 2017 Tax Cuts and Jobs Act, which reduced taxes on the wealthiest below the overall population. This has allowed the top 1% to retain more income and assets. IRS data shows the top 1% income share has nearly doubled from 10% in the 1970s to over 20% today. I suspect that even this statistic is greatly skewed in their favor. However, the wealthy have many tools to increase their net worth in ways not classified as ordinary income, often paying minimal or no taxes. Much of this concentration stems from the richest Americans' stock ownership, with the top 1% owning over 50% of shares in public and private companies, dramatically increasing their net worth.

I worked as a consultant for a wealthy oil man in the mid-80s. He would sit in the morning on the porch of his colonial mansion in Covington, LA, sipping his café au lait, watching his trainers run his thoroughbred horses around the track he had built that circled his massive home. This was his daily routine before his helicopter transported him across the lake to his office in the New Orleans CBD. He was a jovial character, but one day he arrived at his office absolutely furious and screaming at his accountant. I had never seen him like this. A short time later, he called me in to discuss our project. He started venting about his accountant's incompetence, which resulted in a massive $500,000 tax bill for him for the year! I tactfully asked him the details about that tax year. He revealed his income was a bit over $70 million. I pointed out that $500,000 was not even 1% of his income in taxes, and that his accountant must be a wizard. My boss asked me if I was an idiot. He explained that he should not have to pay even $1 in taxes on his level. He never had in the previous decades, but his accountant royally screwed up. I made a low six-figure income that year, and my tax bracket was about 40%.

Even these stories and measures understate the full extent of inequality. Alternative metrics like the Genuine Progress Indicator (GPI) provide a more accurate picture than GDP or income alone. In contrast to GDP's simple aggregation of spending, GPI adjusts for factors like inequality, environmental damage, and household labor. According to GPI metrics analyzed by Friends of the Earth, while

GDP per capita has increased since 1950, GPI per capita peaked in 1978 and has since stagnated or declined. This divergence shows how GDP growth has been powered more by inequality and environmental damage rather than real societal gains. For instance, between 1990 and 2020 GDP per capita grew 75% while GPI per capita, adjusted for worsening inequality, increased only 8%. By incorporating social and environmental impacts, GPI provides a truer measure of welfare over simplistic GDP.

While alternative metrics like GPI offer crucial insights, fundamentally reshaping economic systems also requires structural changes in resource allocation. The extreme concentration of wealth and power among an elite few has created unsustainable imbalances, depriving billions of basic security and opportunity. To build economies centered on equitable distribution necessitates progressive policies to actively redistribute resources, not just different measurement tools.

Redistributive policies that shift wealth, income, and ownership into more balanced configurations can foster broadly shared prosperity. Wealth redistribution provides a pragmatic approach to fund social programs uplifting the poor while restoring greater equality. Implementing interventions like progressive taxes, improved regulation, and new corporate ownership models allows democratically redirecting capital to benefit all.

According to the London School of Economics, redistributive taxes on the wealthiest households could raise $3.75 trillion over 10 years in the U.S. alone, providing universal health care, childcare, paid leave, and more while reducing vast disparities. In the pandemic, the net worth of the wealthiest 25 Americans grew over $400 billion from March to December 2020. A moderate 2% wealth tax on fortunes above $50 million would have raised their tax contribution to the public sector by $60 billion, funding critical needs while leaving ample wealth. Just 1.4% of the richest American families could provide the $117 billion annual investment required to lift every American above poverty. With thoughtful wealth redistribution, we can fund social programs while restoring balance.

In summary, the data makes clear the stark and growing inequality in America, with capitalism in its current form systemically concentrating wealth among the elite few at the expense of the broad populace since the 1970s. Alternative economic metrics accounting for factors beyond GDP also reveal how recent growth has been powered more by inequality and environmental damage rather than real societal gains.

The extreme imbalances of recent decades have created unsustainable disparities depriving billions of security; and more importantly, they are deprived of the means to be able to afford an education to develop their skills and the opportunity to express their value into their chosen profession or vocation. This is underutilizing available resources and manpower, a concept that even a conservative business person should be able to understand. By implementing balanced interventions, capital can be collectively rechanneled to foster shared prosperity and more productivity among a broader majority of our world's population.

The financial hardship that I have had to endure to be able to take the time to write this book and do other work that I believe is important for our society is a perfect example of resource inequality. The people that I know who are drawn to do work for the public good in a direct fashion are almost always driven into extreme poverty. There are no real programs to pay people who are directly focused on helping the environment or creating social systems to make the world more equitable.

When you look past the façade, many people's jobs essentially boil down to providing goods and services that increase convenience, grow the value of investments, or make the wealthy even wealthier. Most endeavors focused on solving major ecological or societal problems are perceived as having little inherent economic value. If you remove the mask of disguise, you find that people are paid to improve the lives of those with means, not to remedy issues facing society as a whole. It is no secret that our system is based on the strategic exploitation of markets and resources.

This stagnation of wages and deprivation of the fundamental resources for so many people who could be enabled to contribute more value is multiplied by the lack of true vision, shared strategic planning, and clear direction. People are lost in this rapidly changing environment that is richly provided with distractions and hurdles. To the degree that wealth and intelligence systems are concentrated among a small fraction of the population, the greater the section of the world's inhabitants that will grapple with abject poverty. Already a majority of the people struggle to survive, even with expanded hourly demands in their work schedules. This trend represents a profound systemic failure and shifts inequities to the point that it cannot sustain even the existing societal health as the approach of the bottom falling out looms closer.

It's startling for me to note that the IRS recently increased the estate-tax exclusion for inherited wealth to $12.92 million. This means a billionaire can pass on $12.92 million to each and every one of their heirs tax-free, even dozens or hundreds of them! Of course, they have tools such as trusts, corporations and other means of passing on far more than a mere $12.92 million to their heirs with little or no tax burdens. Meanwhile, a diligent hard-working family earning an annual income of $150,000 could find themselves in a combined state and federal tax bracket that costs them as much as 40% of their top-bracket income. This state of affairs, favoring the wealthy so disproportionately, strikes me as not only unbalanced but also dangerously skewed.

The practice of accumulating and hoarding wealth intensifies social inequality and obstructs socio-economic mobility. In some societies with socialist policies, the disparity between the wealthiest and poorest members can range from 6 to 10 times. However, in America, this discrepancy can skyrocket to some having millions of times as much money as the poor. Such a pronounced disparity is not only morally dubious but also entirely unsustainable in the long run, paving the way for societal instability and conflict. In the ages gone by, the general population sometimes revolted to take down the overlords. Today the wealthy have beefed up security forces, private mercenaries or police forces, and robotic drone protection. Some are quite prepared to protect what they see as theirs. This extreme imbalance underlines a deeply rooted issue within our current economic framework.

There are many startling examples of where entrenched dynasties have protected their empires, shielding their vast fortunes at the expense of the collective good. My personal journey has seen the protection of entrenched industries create walls of resistance to ward off transformative change that would benefit society on numerous occasions. Here is one such illuminating example:

In the year 1989, within the New Orleans' Superdome, our modest production crew captured Joseph Newman showcasing his groundbreaking energy machine. For the entire day, we illuminated a vast 10,000 square foot room in the dome, with fluorescent lights, and ran household utilities-all clearly suspended on cotton strings to ensure no hidden energy sources. Remarkably, these were energized solely by one of Newman's prototype devices, only slightly larger than a hefty washing machine. The entire setup ran seamlessly for the entire day, kick-started only by a solitary 9-volt flashlight battery to supply the inaugural voltage. Over a thousand spectators, including scientists and engineers, witnessed this marvel, validating its efficacy. The patent office had earlier promised Newman his patent if he successfully demonstrated that his invention generated more energy than it consumed.

However, on the morning of the demonstration, a suspicious government sedan lurked outside our lead producer's residence, culminating in bullets piercing through his front door. Rather than honoring their word, federal agents confiscated Newman's invention. Later, in a horrifying twist, he was apprehended on fabricated allegations, insinuating he had covertly wedded both his new wife and her 8-year-old daughter. Instead of facing prosecution under state laws, he was sequestered in a military research facility at Eglin Air Force Base for over a decade. The man and his groundbreaking invention were systematically obliterated from the public's eye along with any chance of being produced as a clean source of free energy.

In a subsequent sinister episode, unidentified assailants burgled our entire collection of video tapes capturing the event. Given the negligible monetary value of used videotapes, it's reasonable to deduce that the theft was aimed at erasing the documented evidence and preventing us from releasing the documentary.

In our pursuit of the truth, my producer reached out to a close contact within the upper echelons of the NSA and CIA (his father). His unnerving response was unequivocal: dominant powers would never permit such a machine to thrive. Their rationale? In times of upheaval or insurrection, the authorities need to possess the ability to "pull the plug" to shut it all down — a need more pressing than the environment or abundant clean, inexpensive energy for the people of the world.

While this account is particularly alarming, I find it even more alarming that all validation of Newman's invention has been scrubbed from the internet and if you research him, he will simply appear to be another lunatic. I was there and helped hook up the machine. I saw it work. He explained the science to me and what was needed to refine it for consumer use. I believe that if properly refined, this machine could potentially provide the basis for solving many of the energy needs of the world.

In my experience, the Newman energy invention is by no means an isolated incident. As I dug deeper through the spin propaganda, I found other examples of working prototypes of renewable energy devices that faced conspiratorial obstacles to widespread adoption and commercialization.

For instance, Inventor Stanley Meyer produced an electric car powered by water in the 1990s but faced fierce opposition. Eugene Mallove, former MIT Chief Science Writer, alleged resistance from institutions against cold fusion research despite promising early results, and the data showed investment and patents in this field peaked in the 1990s before declining after this industry wide resistance became evident.

Recognizing the monumental environmental and societal benefits of such devices, especially in reducing Earth's greenhouse gases, curbing oil reserve depletion, and reducing nuclear waste accumulation, while working again for CBRE in their capital markets division, I pulled together a soft commitment of over $100 million from some philanthropic investors who expressed interest in backing this challenge. I then set out to champion similar alternative energy inventions. Regrettably, each was invariably shackled with its own story of suppression.

One inventor had developed a working system using hydraulics to push water into a cylinder with small holes under high pressure which made steam. The steam then boosted the pressurized steam through a second cylinder with even smaller holes, resulting in a super-steam, enough to turn an electric turbine. The turbine made enough electricity to keep the system going and have a surplus of electricity for other uses. Again, this was a system that required no outside fuel, except to initially get it going and generated no pollution. This inventor was very difficult to reach; but after a few months, I finally got through under a false name and pretense. When he realized that I was the investor seeking to develop his alternative energy machine, he broke down sobbing and pleaded for me to "Please stop. This invention has been the bane of my existence! I wish I had never discovered the principal. If you knew what you're up against with this, you would never even consider taking it on. I beg you, please, for my sake, your sake, and the sake of my children, drop this, never call again, and forget it even exists. It will never be built! Ever!"

Another sobering perspective was once shared with me by a high-level political consultant. He shared that these innovations threatened industries that rake in $ billions daily. If these industrial behemoths allocated even a mere 1% of their earnings to quell budding competitors, they'd wield over a formidable $30 million per day war chest. Just pondering over those staggering figures and what could be done with such a defense pool made me queasy. He also pointed out that a relative nobody like me with no security protection could probably be killed for under $50 grand. I dropped trying to champion such technologies and moved on.

However, as the aim of this book is not to weave a tale of intrigue, I'll confine our discussion to these few examples and in the following chapter look deeper into the nature of society's capital system disease that alarmingly mimics the nature of cancer.

Yet, even if we can escape the mental traps of accumulation, reshuffling material wealth alone will not be sufficient. Our own inner psyche drives us to "get ahead," to exploit and compete in ways that replicate the very systems we decry. We have to dig deep into our consciousness, uprooting the memes of selfishness. And we cannot excavate too deeply into our collective psyches before we discover there is a pink elephant loitering in the garden of our internal physiological societal belief system, trampling the crops and destroying the landscape.

The Pink Elephant in the Room

Of all the challenges and existential threats humanity faces, the tendency to overpopulate looms as the proverbial elephant in the room. However, deep taboos often prevent meaningful discourse on this topic. Without examining this deal-breaker element of the equation, we would long be pointing out at the other problematic situations, even as overpopulation tramples the very resources and ecosystems that sustain us. Let us look at this quandary with some objectivity and factor what we can discern into the overall mix.

As a species, we are clearly sensual and sexual beings, drawn to breed, and as a result, reproduce, often overlooking or romanticizing the broader implications of continued population growth. Driven by biological urges and cultural norms, we continue to increase our global population unsustainably, while not fully addressing the problematic results, such as resource scarcity, habitat destruction, and intensified climate change.

For most of human history, harsh conditions like wilderness, pestilence, plagues, and war kept our population growth in check, preventing overbreeding within local regions. However, advancing technology and social progress have now insulated humanity from many of these natural checks on our numbers. As a result, the global population has swelled relatively unabated by historical standards. In the past, excessive growth would lead to the collapse of localized civilizations that overburdened their immediate surroundings. Where previously isolated communities would bear the consequences of their growth, today, our unchecked proliferation threatens to collapse our entire planetary ecosystem.

Some may proffer draconian solutions like sterilization, war, or pandemics. However coercive policies that violate human rights are untenable. What we need is a mindset shift at the cultural and individual level. We must elevate the ethos of quality over quantity, where every life brought forth is done consciously, ethically, and with reverence for its impact.

Undoubtedly, instilling discipline around reproduction may be humankind's sternest test yet. But unless we overcome biological urges with moral and ethical ones, our unchecked breeding will breed collective destruction. The time has come to stop ignoring this elephant, and consciously restrict our proliferation to within sustainable bounds. Our future depends on embracing restraint today so that generations tomorrow may live and thrive in balance with our planet.

Rumblings abound of an imposed culling by the oligarchy, a dystopian attempt to violently rip society below a 1 billion population. While overpopulation poses grave risks, such totalitarian methods would inflict tremendous suffering, making the cure worse than the disease. There is a more enlightened path.

Rather than harsh reductions forced upon the masses, we must take collective responsibility for sustainable propagation. By comprehensively revamping systems — from education to economics — we can instill an ethos valuing quality of life over quantity. Policies like family planning support, incentivizing smaller families, and promoting adoption over birthing can help balance numbers ethically.

Concurrently, the large pool of human potential we temporarily have provides an opportunity to redirect efforts toward ecological restoration, regenerating over-farmed land, reforesting degraded zones, and cleaning pollution. Instead of drastic cuts in the near term, gradual demographic shifts coupled with harnessing our resources for planetary healing could achieve balance humanely.

This transition requires maturity to override primal urges with a social conscience. But we must grow beyond isolated genes viewing reproduction as self-propagation. With compassion and collective care, we can create a sustainable future, avoiding fear-based decimation. Our greatness lies not in numbers but in the enduring legacy we build by uplifting all life.

When confronting complex issues like overpopulation, some may object based on religious or spiritual grounds. They may feel reproducing abundantly is their duty, or that limiting family size contradicts their faith. However, looking deeper, most religions share common values of compassion, moderation, and collective responsibility that align with sustainable propagation.

Certainly, many beliefs differ on the surface. Pro-lifers are on one side. Pro-choice on the other. Both are sure they are right, each convinced the "true" God is on their side. But peering beneath belief differences, deep into the gem of God, both sides try to support what they believe is true and moral. The direction may seem opposite, but the divine essence they worship is strikingly similar — an omniscient force of creation, offering divine love and truth.

As we move deeper into unhealthy restraints, let's unravel and examine some more of the specific unhealthy dynamics of capitalism. It will be helpful to draw some parallels with similar dynamics and systems in the natural world. A few years back, I talked with a friend about his fight with cancer. The more I listened, the more it occurred to me how similar it sounded to the growing dynamics of capitalism in our global society. Later I researched the similarities, and the deeper I looked, the more astonished I was to see the parallels between the growth of cancer within the human body and what is happening economically in our system.

In the ensuing section, we will drill deeper into this dynamic, exploring the stark parallels between cancerous growth and unchecked capitalism, and their shared destructive patterns. We'll also examine the means by which we can refocus and redirect this growth toward a healthier, better functioning, equitable future.

V.
The Cancer of Crony Capitalism: A Striking Analogy

Challenges to systemic change in America are deeply entrenched within our monetary capitalist system. The grip of "Big Money" and its vast influence perpetuates these challenges, steering the system in manifold ways. Over time, I've come to view the tactics of the wealthy oligarchy as mirroring the insidious nature of cancer cells as they take over a body. Upon further reflection and analysis, I found this analogy deeply and disturbingly parallel.

Viewed in this light, the excessive accumulation of wealth and influence by modern corporate and financial elites could be seen as a form of cultural Wetiko. When profit motives override all other values and insatiable appetites control economies and governments, the common good becomes consumed. Recognizing these cannibalistic tendencies may be the first step in restoring balance, ensuring vitality and abundance for all rather than enriching only a few.

The insatiable desire to "get ahead" and the influence "Big Money" wields within our "crony" style capitalist framework closely mirrors the progression and dominance of cancer. On a physiological level.

Much like a malignant tumor grows unchecked, usurping healthy tissue and commandeering resources for its proliferation, unrestrained greed similarly devours resources and amasses wealth like tumors. The similarities are chilling, painting a vivid picture of the dangers of unchecked expansion of personal fortunes and corporate interests. In a similar light, the continuous accumulation of wealth and the expanding resource divide can be likened to a tumor manipulating its surroundings, ensuring its growth and sustenance, thereby leading to systemic imbalances and malfunction.

However, let me be clear; this metaphor is not to demonize capitalism or overlook the many technological and beneficial contributions that ingenious industrialists, wealthy innovators, or companies have been responsible for championing, but rather to illuminate the areas where intervention and reform are urgently needed. Much like diagnosing cancer allows us to develop targeted treatments, identifying these issues in our economic system provides us with the opportunity to address them head-on.

In this section, we will explore this metaphor, examining the parallels between the stages of cancer progression and the problems inherent in our capitalist system. We will examine cancer-like parallels, such as invasive growth and its equivalent in campaign bribery or lobbying; the induction of angiogenesis and its parallels in redirecting resources; and the consumptive growth inherent in passive wealth accumulation. By drawing these parallels, I aim to highlight the urgent need for a recalibration of our economic system — one that fosters sustainability, equity, and a renewed respect for our planet. The path to such a transformation may not be easy, but as we will discuss, alternatives exist, and the potential for change is within our grasp.

There is a striking correlation between cancer's destructive biology and the systemic repercussions of uncontrolled capitalism that could indeed form the basis of an in-depth book. We will endeavor to encapsulate some of the key similarities in this analogy, illustrating how unchecked capitalism can eerily mirror the rampant growth and impact of cancer.

Uncontrolled Growth: Cancer involves the uncontrollable and rapid growth of abnormal cells. These cells proliferate relentlessly, ignoring the biological controls that normally regulate cell growth and division.

Capitalist Correlation — Runaway Capital Accumulation: Much like the uncontrolled growth of cancer cells and how it spreads into other systems of the body, capitalism often leads to the relentless accumulation of capital which is accomplished by playing with or even controlling political and economic systems. The primary motivation in capitalism is the maximization of profit and accumulation of more capital and assets, with less regard for the system's overall health.

The uncontrolled growth of capital often lacks a consideration of the social and environmental impacts, similar to cancer cells disregarding the health of the organism they inhabit. Those who live off of accumulated wealth, playing "the money game" rather than providing essential products or services to society may actually cause damage. It leads to creating wall-street strategies like the failed derivative securities, the CMBS market, or bundled subpar mortgages.

On the levels of oligarchy, these regimes are known to sell arms, start wars to increase market demand, sabotage infrastructure, derail education and humane efforts; all ways to generate revenue and profit, while hurting society. Just as cancer cells selfishly reroute blood supply and absorb excess resources to feed unrestrained growth of tumors while starving beneficial organs, the capitalist profit motive often directs resources towards them, while starving the working class. An example of this might be the huge disparity of Covid subsidies towards the wealthy, and the damaging policies directed to shut down small businesses and stop people from working. These policies help mega businesses, like Amazon, but are often antithetical to the common good of society.

There are more parallels than these I included here, but I am focusing on the more important ones, which are:

Non-Beneficial Allocation of Resources: In cancer, the body's resources are hijacked to fuel the growth of cancer cells. These cells take up nutrients and space, diverting resources away from normal cells and functions.

Capitalist Correlation — Wealth Hoarding: In capitalism, a similar non-beneficial allocation of resources can be observed. The wealthy minority often accumulates and hoards resources at the expense of the majority. This wealth hoarding starves other sectors of society of needed resources and opportunities, reminiscent of how cancer cells deprive normal cells. One example might be my estimate of how the subsidies for COVID-19 were allocated over 10 to 1 towards the wealthy and business owners.

Resistance to Apoptosis (Programmed Cell Death)/Corporations: Cell death is a valuable part of reducing disease and remaining youthful. Cancer cells resist apoptosis, a mechanism that causes damaged or harmful cells to self-destruct. This resistance allows cancer cells to survive and proliferate even when they are perverted and harm the body.

Capitalist Correlation — Corporate Immortality: Corporations and estates, under capitalism, exhibit a similar resistance to "death." Despite causing harm to society or the environment, corporations and estates resist death and pass on power and wealth indefinitely. They are structured to prioritize their own survival and growth over the well-being of the larger system, often avoiding even basic taxes as they seed the next generation with their wealth.

Metastasis: Cancer not only grows in one place, it frees up cells and spreads them to grow in other parts of the body through a process called metastasis. This enables the cancer to infiltrate new systems and makes the disease much harder to treat and control.

Capitalist Correlation — Globalization of Exploitative Practices: Similarly, harmful practices within capitalism can spread across borders, industries, political lines, and more, much like metastasis. Unregulated capitalism tends to export exploitative labor practices, environmental destruction, bid and market rigging, and economic disparities to other regions and countries.

Evasion of the Immune System: A defining feature of cancer is its ability to evade the body's immune system. By doing so, it can continue to grow and spread without being destroyed by the body's defenses.

Capitalist Correlation — Evasion of Regulatory Systems: In the world of capitalism, similar evasion tactics can be seen in how they instill agents in police forces, and military and political structures. Corporations often pay huge lobbyist fees, and campaign contributions or find other ways to circumvent or weaken regulatory systems designed to curb harmful practices and maintain economic balance.

These are just a few of the examples of the cancer-capitalism metaphor. We are not really touching on the use of *toxicity*, *induced angiogenesis*, *microenvironment modification*, *invasive growth*, and *consumptive growth parallels*. Each of these would provide even further insight into how unregulated, runaway capitalism mirrors the growth and impact of cancer. For now, we will skip ahead to look at how to help heal the systemic invasion.

Potential Reforms and Alternatives

Cancer, known for its virulence and relentless survival instincts, often leads to the patient's death due to its aggressive campaign for existence. Now, please hear me when I say that I am not suggesting that capitalistic cancer could kill society. It's not like the ruling powers have built some sort of a doomsday device where someone could kill off the masses with the push of a button if their power and amassed wealth were in jeopardy. Of course, they would be killing themselves as well.

They would need underground bunkers and years of supplies to survive such a holocaust. Nobody thinks that far ahead, so I will not state such an implausible notion.

Cancer, however, does not need to be able to kill the body all at once. It sustains the body in a state where it can feed off of it. Its goal is not to kill the body, yet often it is fatal. It wields a vast array of devastating tools, causing imbalance and dysfunction to support its continued growth. It hijacks the blood supply by taking over normal system intelligence and disrupting functions by creating distraction, sedation, and confusion. Cancer can manipulate healthy cells by doping them up and disrupting the body's natural intelligence and ability to operate its crucial systems. Can you think of similar dynamics in our current system?

My two teenage boys and I live in Phoenix now. Recently I met a very interesting gentleman while looking for compost to amend our dirt into soil so I can start a garden. I crave a good source of fresh organic greens and they are too pricey for my budget. Ken Singh owns Singh Meadows and Singh Farms, one of the few remaining family-owned and operated farms in the Phoenix, Scottsdale, and Tempe, Arizona areas. They still grow and sell fresh, organic produce and host various events and activities for the community. I was delighted to get some great compost and have the opportunity to listen to this very knowledgeable person, who has farmed the area, taught by his father, using natural farming methods for his entire lifetime — since before the term 'permaculture' even existed.

To my surprise, Ken told me that the Phoenix area, known as "The Valley of the Sun," was once a very fertile growing region. From early on and through the 70s, it was ranked among the top five produce-growing areas in America. He explained that, several decades ago, the influx of big-money developers exerted their political control and decided to convert most of the farmlands into housing developments. Ken tried to reason with their big-money agenda, primarily because he knew that eating food grown within 150 miles of where you live boosts your natural immunities, but his attempt to save farmlands was not effective. The lure of abundant short-term wealth overcame the community leaders' innate survival intelligence to maintain a reasonable balance of sustainable food production in the area.

The shift away from plant-ground covering in favor of more roads, paving, and roof tiles has significantly elevated temperatures over the past 50 years. When I arrived at my new home in mid-July, the high temperatures were between 115° and 122° every day for 6 weeks. This raised sobering questions for me. If there was a shutdown of the supply grid in the summer, what would we do? How long would this city survive without deliveries and power? If the food trucks stopped delivering? Clearly, this community can no longer come even close to feeding itself from the surrounding area. What if the utilities went off? People can not live in these summer temperatures without air conditioning. If this were part of a larger meltdown, would the highways be locked down to prevent the chaos of people desperately fleeing? How long would we be able to survive? Weeks or less?

Will capitalism's cancer-like shutdown of rational survival planning in favor of wealth accumulation similarly threaten other metropolitan areas? How long will NY, LA, or other concentrated metropolitan areas survive if the big machine stops chugging? A few weeks? More or less? Just how dependent are we on this unsustainable system? How far out on a limb have we climbed? How grave is this issue? Could the defense mechanisms of amassed and growing tumors of fortunes and their pursuit of unchecked power pull us into our annihilation? Would there even be weapons to destroy civilization?

In my view, this issue of controlling and misappropriating resources to starve off healthy cells, while containing or distorting intelligent planning by healthy cells is among the gravest and most challenging problems humanity has ever faced. It perverts those who have a true intention to focus their lives and careers on improving the health of the ecosystem and society in general. This process lies at the heart of how cancer invades and pervades a human body, by controlling and weakening the body's natural defense system and healthy organ functions. On a societal level, the same parallel dynamic distorts our ability to handle some of our most significant challenges by depleting the resources of those who are willing to tackle the challenges. The cancer cells often intentionally stand as roadblocks preventing the real problems from being properly addressed and remedied. Medical science has devised treatments targeting cancer, offering hope of recovery. In parallel, we can develop treatments for cancerous traits of unchecked capitalism.

It is nothing new to human society that those in power can remove those governing authorities who challenge their regimes and reward those who overlook or support their activities. Monarchies and dictatorships have realigned opposition for millennia. The main difference now is the stakes are vastly larger. It is no longer a turf war for a limited geographic area. It is a global tug-of-war that threatens everyone in the world, whether they know it or not.

Those who threaten national and international governments, big business, and security agencies whose job is to protect the interests of the oligarchy have shifted from terrorists to activists trying to make a positive difference. The expanded list now includes many environmentalists, natural healers who would treat cancer or COVID-19, social evolutionaries, visionaries, and spiritual leaders. They seem to be threatened by some of those who strive to make the greatest direct contributions to humanity because their work and narrative are in opposition to the over-exploitation of the world's resources and destructive industries.

Before his assassination, John Lennon was considered to be one of the most dangerous men on Earth by certain government enforcement agencies. Did they kill him? Some are sure they did orchestrate it. Others who are rumored to be threatened include Osho, much of the Kennedy clan, Greta Thunberg, George Harrison — I have my own personal experiences, as well — and *many* more. The list is extremely long.

All of life as we know it faces the risk of total collapse and annihilation if we do not stand up as a people. We must usher in an age where we support reasonable, intelligent planning that directly addresses the very serious and real issues that threaten us. First and foremost, we must preserve the delicate ecology of the planet. The Earth provides for the survival of all of the life that inhabits her, including humans. The other social and economic problems are important, but if the ecosystem collapses, we will not have the time to solve the others.

This has become an All or Nothing Game between white-fisted knuckles of control, and those who are willing to fight for a better way. Like Greta Thunberg, we did not want this. They have pulled us into this arena to compete for the survival and future of the people of Earth. We simply cannot blind ourselves to the truth. The truth is that all of us, irrespective of our self-interests, are uniquely gifted creative beings, born of stardust. We are Children of the Most High, God's beloved family, one people. We need to recognize this truth more fully.

We need to engage the full power of the Crew of Spaceship Earth to create in-depth logistics for specific solutions. Together, we will recognize these cancer-like traits in our economic system, and explore and refine potential reforms. As a collective, we will act on alternatives and redirect society towards healthier, more sustainable, and equitable models. Certainly, if I had even one month working with the Crew of Spaceship Earth and a suitable AI platform to synergize and model these high-altitude plans, the result would make the following suggestions pale in comparison. My goal is not to convince anyone that I have all the answers but to inspire you to realize that we as a collective force can create the solutions we need to these pressing problems that are going largely unaddressed.

Uncontrolled Growth: Instilling regulatory policies that limit unchecked growth and promote sustainable business practices is paramount. For instance, mandating corporate social responsibility (CSR) and initiatives can be an effective way of ensuring companies invest in sustainable growth, balancing their profit drive with social and environmental welfare.

Non-Beneficial Allocation of Resources: To counteract the detrimental allocation of resources, we need to encourage responsible investing and consumption. This might involve promoting businesses that prioritize ethical and sustainable practices, thereby aligning resource allocation with societal and environmental needs. Certainly, AI could help with the logistics if allowed to engage in such a truly beneficial equation.

Resistance to Apoptosis/Corporations: Just as apoptosis regulates cell life, we must regulate corporations' lifespans and ranges of influence. This could mean implementing stringent antitrust laws to prevent monopolistic tendencies and promote market competition, thus ensuring economic diversity and vibrancy. In addition, significantly reducing the ability to pass on family fortunes is essential through reasonable, yet significant inheritance laws, stringent trust regulations, and imposing significant inheritance taxes. I would suggest no less than 50% inheritance taxes.

Wealth Hoarding and Parallels in Cancer: Just as cancer tumors accumulate resources, wealth accumulation can cause economic disparities. Most people believe rich people do not pay taxes, just as Donald Trump, a billionaire, pays less than a modestly employed family. To combat this, we need progressive taxation that taxes the wealthy at higher rates, encouraging a more equitable distribution of resources.

Metastasis: To mitigate economic metastasis — where wealth continually concentrates in certain sectors or regions, such as blood flow to tumors — we need policies encouraging wealth redistribution and regional development. This could involve progressive taxation or investment in underdeveloped areas.

Evasion of the Immune System: To tackle the issue of corporations and dynasties evading regulatory "immune systems," we need robust, transparent, and accountable regulatory bodies. By strengthening institutional integrity, we can ensure corporations are held to account.

Toxicity, Pain to Distract and Control: To counteract the distracting pain caused by economic hardship, we need comprehensive welfare systems that protect society's most vulnerable. By ensuring everyone has access to services and resources essential to aiding them in becoming their most prolific contributors, we can build a more resilient society.

Induction of Angiogenesis: Instead of enabling industries to manipulate and monopolize resources (economic "blood supply"), we should promote resource conservation and efficient use. This could involve supporting renewable energy sources over fossil fuels.

Microenvironment Modification: To combat the harmful modification of economic "microenvironments," we need to protect and promote local economies and small businesses. By supporting local initiatives, we can help maintain economic diversity and resilience.

Invasive Growth and Impairment of Function: To fight against the "invasive growth" of corporate power and influence, we need to enforce strict lobbying and bribery laws. This could help ensure policy-making remains in the hands of democratically elected representatives, not wealthy corporations.

Consumptive Growth and the Perils of Passive Wealth: We need to encourage active, productive use of wealth rather than passive accumulation. This could involve taxing or expiring unproductive wealth or offering tax incentives for investments in social goods.

In our endeavor to mitigate unchecked capitalism, we can find inspiration from the methods employed to combat cancer. Our goal is to redirect growth towards a more balanced, sustainable, and equitable model. This shift won't be without its challenges. The privileged, **Super-Wealth Class — comprising far less than 1% of the population** — may not willingly forfeit their positions of power. Their influence is largely predicated on maintaining control through the tactical distribution of resources and their enforcers. However, as society becomes increasingly cognizant of the unsustainable burden this places on the majority, support for this power structure is likely to wane.

In my view, a significant catalyst for change will emerge when those within the intelligence communities and control structures — serving as lieutenants to these modern-day Pharaohs, corporations, and oligarchies — recognize the immense cost of enforcing policies that benefit a tiny fraction at the expense of the world. When they fully realize that their orders are detrimental to society at large, and their own families, friends, and themselves, some will shift their allegiance and turn their focus onto the real criminals that run the rackets from the top.

However, focusing solely on the economic elite obscures a deeper truth — the capitalistic cancer takes root not just in society, but in our collective psyche. We need to look at ourselves, not just the super-rich who pervert the health of the system.

Earlier we mentioned the Cree concept of Wetiko, which was defined as a "cannibal sickness." This term provides an illuminating metaphor. Wetiko was seen as a disease of the spirit that drove selfish consumption and greed at the expense of the community. Just as a literal cannibal consumes the flesh of others to feed their own appetite, those afflicted with Wetiko are possessed by a never-ending hunger for wealth, power, and control which consumes the tribal body. Their pursuit of more comes at a great cost, draining resources and fracturing social bonds. Much like a cancer that metastasizes throughout the body, the grasping force of Wetiko spreads far beyond the afflicted individual, undermining the overall health of tribes and nations when left unchecked.

While today we have corporations and estates that can focus the profit motive into collectives, we might deduce that this same shift may happen within us individually. When our supporting faculties of reason recognize that serving the tyrannical demands of unhealthy egos does not serve our greater good, we may shift our allegiance to the ways of the dark ego. Within this pivot may reside the promise of more rational, and healthy people who make better decisions for their own well-being and all those aboard Spaceship Earth.

The Pursuit of Wealth Over Purpose

Money at its best is a currency able to fuel health and provide the basic needs of all the cells so they can perform their designated and valuable function, contributing to the collective health to enrich society.

In a cancerous body, the cancer cells feed the healthy cells chemicals and sedatives to weaken their opposition. In a usurped economic system, the otherwise healthy members are strategically fed distractions, drugs, false models, and propaganda. These belief systems encourage them to foolishly go for the gold ring, believing they may be the next big winners of passive wealth. We are misled to support the capital accumulation system by the puppeteering of master marketing executives, media, public leaders, and their policies. When profit rules over purpose, the result is akin to malignant tumors interfering with the body's natural intelligence and regulation.

This disease infiltrates our collective thinking from the wealthiest to the poorest of people. Just as cancer cells selfishly absorb resources to feed unrestrained growth, the capitalist profit motive often drives the decisions of individuals on all socioeconomic levels. We are convinced that accumulating wealth is more important than even supporting our species' ability to survive for more than a few more generations. Many people simply do not have the time, focus, or interest to address our collective self-preservation, the needs of the environment, or social projects that are in the best interest of our collective well-being. They must make more money.

We can see this dynamic in indirect forms, such as street gangs who push drugs on their own already disadvantaged people, or as seemingly innocuous as impoverished people spending much of their limited income on lotto tickets or other forms of gambling to get ahead when the odds are clearly stacked against them.

An ideal system would create conditions for individuals to fully express their talents and innovations for society's advancement without them having to be wealthy enough to pay for the opportunity they cannot afford. The opportunities would be provided by the society that wants its people to be able to contribute their full value to the collective.

When we look more deeply at the pursuit of wealth over the purpose of directing labor to improve our environment, society, and world management systems, we can see how it leads directly to societal organ failure. The parallel is very similar to cancer's unchecked growth through impairing the function of bodily organs, whose job would include fighting the cancer. Just as cancer can lead to organ failure in the body, the uncontrolled pursuit of wealth, even when it is never obtained, can cause our society's intelligence and planning process to break down on an individual and collective level in very critical ways.

Many young people today feel they must pursue financially lucrative careers, sometimes at the expense of seeking roles that align with their genuine talents and passions. There's a prevailing sentiment that pursuing one's true calling might not enable their financial well-being or stability. This can be likened to the body's natural wisdom being overshadowed by tools of cancer.

Instead of primarily focusing on making money, why don't we channel our youth's efforts towards enhancing food quality, fostering vibrant communities, innovating clean energy, producing enriching art and literature, advancing medical practices, cultivating expert technicians and professionals? The intrinsic value of these pursuits should far surpass the allure of roles that prioritize profit over genuine societal contributions. These expressions and paths have more real and tangible value than making money as a Wall Street con artist, a corrupt politician, or a marketing guru who bends your desires to want something you don't need.

Planetary health is also being neglected as resources are channeled towards other dimensions of our lifestyles — such as a convenient, yet disposable single-use reality or plug-and-play component manufacturing that prevents repairs and maintenance of devices. It is not just profit over stewardship that disrupts the natural functions of our culture. Just as cancer diverts nutrients from healthy cells, the drive to succeed, to get a more luxurious ride that wealth offers, diverts our focus. We even scoff at people who discuss the need to take action that is urgently needed to help ensure our species' survival. It is fashionable to overlook our planetary stability in favor of getting ahead, being prestigious and fresh. Activities, such as regenerating forests and tending the health of the earth are for people below or above their station. Someone else can and will do it. Or so they say to avoid making their needed contributions.

Institutions that support their industry's cash flow over what contributes to the greater good are numerous. Here are a few examples:

- America promotes its high-gluten wheat even though it creates inflammation and disease. European countries have outlawed this horrible hybrid wheat, but America forces it down our throats.
- Cardiologists are not allowed to discuss or recommend using EDTA, which can clear away an arterial blockage, but it also eliminates the need for most stents or bypass operations.
- Pesticides and poisons are promoted and even subsidized as solutions when clearly they are now a bigger problem than bugs or weeds.
- MSG and other additives are in almost every fast and processed food even though science has revealed that they trigger unhealthy food addictions, and cause obesity and many other health problems.
- Genetic modification programs are economically supported and supplemented at the expense of localized farming and heirloom seeds, which are under siege. Roundup Ready crops are a perfect example of this madness.
- Pharmaceuticals are given high priority while natural remedies that are effective and far less expensive are blocked and discredited.

- Political systems are entrenched with corporate alliances that keep the compromised good ol' boys of destruction in power.
- War and weapons manufacturing is a massive multi-trillion-dollar industry.
- Clean alternative energy systems are quelled and blocked so oil and nuclear can generate billions a day for these industry tycoons, despite the cataclysmic problems they create.
- Movie stars are cast in roles that glorify the three big F's: f**king, fighting, and finance. They live exorbitant lifestyles, while they fire many bullets, exploit women and create a massive wake of destruction behind them. All the while, "saving the world!" These plots create destructive role models and false images of what is really important to our young and impressionable audiences.

The examples could be listed in huge volumes, and it is apparent that our collective intelligence is being usurped and misdirected. Meanwhile, vital societal systems are corrupted by corporate motivations, while greed infiltrates a deeper part of each of us and our thinking.

In the body, cancer forces normal cells to support and fuel its unchecked growth. In society, the cancerous institutions of massive wealth commandeer many people's navigation, talents, and resources to protect their unbridled expansion, leading to a breakdown of vital decision-making systems essential to our collective well-being.

To create a healthy society, we must transition back from an economic and personal perspective centered around wealth accumulation and towards providing fulfilling life paths that focus on a rich fabric of life and a society that is healthy and balanced.

Treating the Cancer Within Us

As we acknowledge the inherent issues with a system that fosters an excessive concentration of wealth, it becomes evident that this problem is not only significant but also pervasive. The pursuit of wealth and passive income infiltrates our mindset, transcending economic levels. Addressing this matter is of utmost importance. In the following chapters, I will revisit key dynamics and explore potential remedies to this widespread influence.

The wealth gap is a symptom of a cultural malady that prizes profits and accumulation above the value of people and the planet. The capitalists we should be most concerned about are not just those with billions in assets, but the entrenched mindset within each of us. Like cancer duping healthy cells to aid its growth, unbridled capitalism distracts us with lottery dreams and gold-ring aspirations. It seduces us to play the game, falsely promising that this time we'll be the winners, the victors who can finally do good.

In pursuing these fleeting carrots of wealth and power, we neglect our true calling — to evolve beyond shallow greed and discover our innate passion for adding value to the world. We relinquish "being the change" we wish to see in the world.

A system that prioritizes profit over purpose is akin to a cancer that distorts healthy cells from fulfilling their vital roles in sustaining the body. In an ideal economy, individuals should be empowered to fully contribute their talents to the betterment of society. Unfortunately, entrenched capitalism has evolved into a destructive tumor, seizing control of society's resources.

VI.
EMBRACING SPACESHIP EARTH ETHICS

I struggled for many years to more fully embrace the paradigm shift from my previous belief in the need to make money to being able to recognize the value of my true nature. I have to work to align my ability to express goodness in life. It is not easy for me to recognize that expressing my inner vision is my most reliable source of attaining the means I require for survival.

Whenever I backpedaled into my old paradigm to create "financial security," my venture would inevitably melt down. Often, the meltdowns seemed bigger than me, such as during 9/11 or COVID-19, which both obliterated ventures that looked promising. Invariably, I was reminded my path is now in a different direction. My security comes in the form of my relationship with Source, *not* my accumulation of money.

It takes trust for me to be gentle and generous when I have been taught it's a dog-eat-dog world. It requires a state of personal and collective evolution to be able to contribute value into a shared bounty and trust that we will be provided for based on our contributions. Sometimes business seems like a poker game and when the chips hit the table, hands grab for the pot. Those who are less aggressive are often left with nothing. As the shift in consciousness moves more towards collective contribution, we will naturally be able to relax and be confident that contributing our value will result in obtaining what we need to survive and thrive.

The more we recognize how the interconnected web of Earth's support provides for all her various expressions of life, the more clearly we will reframe our relationship with each other and with Spaceship Earth — from her being a mere repository of resources to be exploited into revering her as a vibrant, living organism that sustains and nurtures us all. This renewed "awakened" perspective invokes a profound sense of responsibility toward our planet, guiding our decisions towards honoring and preserving her delicate balance.

As we shift our mindset from a focus on winning to one centered on contributing value, from consuming resources to embracing reciprocity, and from indifference to compassion, a natural evolution occurs — we become stewards of Earth. Radiating our unique abilities and expressing nurturing energies outward, we recognize that beyond the essential necessities for survival, such as minimal food and shelter, the significance lies in what we contribute as creative expression. While survival dictates the basics of our existence, it's our creative expression that truly defines our humanity.

Throughout human history, we've largely been driven by an ethos of outer conquest. We've sought to command, control, and extract whatever we want or need from the Earth's bounty, often with scant regard for the consequences. While this mindset has indeed propelled us to remarkable technological advancements, material accumulation, and consumption, it has simultaneously birthed environmental degradation, social inequity, and an unsettling disconnection from our natural world.

In our current epoch, many people are coming to realize that this mode of operation is not just unsustainable, but also detrimental to our personal evolution, our emotional and mental health, and to the harmonious existence of all life on Spaceship Earth. The time for conquering, for keeping score in material wealth, is over; the era of nurturing our deeper selves beckons us.

Redefining Wealth

The Transformational journey calls for a profound reevaluation of our understanding of "wealth." Rather than viewing it as an accumulation of material possessions, we begin to equate wealth with personal growth and fulfillment, the richness of our relationships and experiences, and the positive impact we can have on the world. This shift has the potential to bring about transformative change in our society when people aspire not to hoard and accumulate but to contribute and co-create.

Navigating this paradigm shift poses significant challenges, especially for those deeply rooted in the belief that their identities are intertwined with their material wealth. Our current societal structures, which have evolved to a point where power and influence are often linked with monetary assets, further complicate this transition.

Individuals with extensive resources, having secured significant footholds in policy-making and societal control mechanisms, might find detaching from these anchors daunting. It's essential to approach such individuals with empathy and understanding, recognizing the profound introspection and courage it demands to see beyond net worth as a sole indicator of life's value.

However, as this evolved perspective permeates our consciousness and as societal systems adapt to ensure everyone's fundamental needs are met, the compulsion to hoard diminishes. We begin to realize that true value resides not in financial assets but in the richness of our experiences and the positive footprints we leave behind. Moreover, by cherishing and tending to our Earth, we foster a reciprocal relationship where its abundant resources are generously shared, ensuring prosperity for all.

Embracing Minimalism

By placing value on personal evolution and experiences, we are encouraged to consume only what is necessary. Similar to how a vehicle needs just enough fuel to run, we only need enough to maintain our health, clothe and house ourselves, and support our life's work. This minimalist approach not only diminishes our environmental footprint but also frees us from the shackles of consumerism, allowing us to live more meaningful and fulfilling lives.

In this nurturing paradigm, giving more than we take becomes a societal norm, creating an environment of shared abundance. Just as a river that overflows its banks doesn't lose its vitality but instead nourishes the lands around it, our generosity doesn't deplete us but enriches our communities.

Minimalism isn't just about having fewer possessions. It is a holistic approach that encourages the removal of unnecessary distractions and focuses on what truly adds value to one's life. This principle is so key and essential that we will look a little deeper at some benefits of adopting a minimalist lifestyle, including:

A Clearer Mind and Increased Focus: By decluttering our space and commitments, we can reduce decision fatigue and focus on tasks that truly matter.

Financial Freedom: With fewer desires to buy and accumulate, we often save more and reduce financial stress.

Increased Time: By prioritizing essential tasks and eliminating excess, we gain more time to invest in hobbies, relationships, and self-care.

Greater Appreciation: When we have fewer things, we tend to value and appreciate what we do have more.

Reduced Environmental Footprint: Owning and consuming less results in a reduced environmental impact.

Simplified Living: Life becomes more straightforward and less stressful when we're not overwhelmed maintaining possessions, meeting superfluous obligations, or tending to unnecessary commitments.

Enhanced Well-being: As Zen philosophy eloquently expresses, "a clean and decluttered space results in a decluttered mind," reducing anxiety and leading to increased well-being.

Improvement in Relationships: When materialism is not the core focus, we tend to value and prioritize our relationships more.

Boosted Productivity: With fewer distractions, our efficiency and productivity often see a marked improvement.

From Consumption to Creative Expression

The more I have focused on developing my creativity and personal expression, the more I have become aware of how personal indulgence and sensory stimulation are distractions to my ability to deeply focus and express clear intentions in my thinking, art and life in general. An example of this might be when, in the late '80s and '90s, I worked on many major label music videos and often got to meet the artists; many of them listen to very little music from other artists because it dilutes their ability to hear their own source of music.

The personal developmental path I am suggesting is not of doing without, but more of discovering the greater value that is inherent within us. It is the process of learning what is really important and living more abundantly through refocusing on our expressions rather than our consumption.

The essence of life isn't just about what we take in — be it food, knowledge, or experiences; it's about contributing, transforming, and radiating our unique perspectives and energies outward. Taking in may fuel our bodies and minds, yet, it's what we manifest and express outwardly from that nourishment, through our thoughts, actions, and creations, that is our contribution in the world, and is said to be the only expression that remains here on our soul's timeless journey. Just as a tree absorbs nutrients to bloom and bear fruit, we, too, are enriched by our experiences so we can offer something unique and valuable in return. While survival dictates the basics of our existence, it's our creative expression that truly defines our humanity.

I have heard and even believe that the destruction and damage we have caused to the Earth through the phases of our development can be well justified and even welcomed as a price well worth paying if the flower of our soul unfolds its full blossom. However, for us to have the time and space to mature fully so that we can make our highest expressions as a species, we will have to tend to the Earth's needs and each other so we have a home in which to evolve.

In the Hindu religion, it is said that the Earth is a mid-planet between Heavenly and Hellish worlds, and therefore the perfect school for soul evolution. The Heavenly planets are too pleasurable for their inhabitants to concern themselves with change or growth, while the hellish worlds torment their inhabitants so much that personal suffering becomes an obstacle to any real growth. Furthermore, we are in the perfect place for growth and should utilize every minute we have and take advantage of the benefits we can achieve on a soul level. They say that the demand to be on this Earth is so great among souls that to win a spot in the body here is approximately like winning a lotto with 5 billion other souls competing for the spot. Yet, if this is true, most of us surely take it for granted.

From Outer Conquering to Inner Nurturing

It was not so long ago that humans had to carve out their space from a fierce and dangerous wilderness, so it is not surprising that we have come to see the world around us as an arena to conquer and establish our dominion. Yet, as we stand at the crossroads of our evolution, there's a growing realization that this time has passed and now the quest is for true discovery, not just in the expanse of the universe, but deep within the depth of our own selves, our unconscious minds, our soul.

The external world we see today, in many ways, is a mirror. It reflects the collective psyche of humanity, representing both our aspirations and our shadows. The conflicts, the advancements, the problems we tackle are manifestations of our internal struggles. Millennia of conditioning have propelled us to believe that acquisition is the key to happiness - be it territories, wealth, relationships or knowledge. And while such pursuits had their place in our evolutionary journey, there comes a point of saturation; a point where accumulation no longer quenches our thirst, and we're compelled to introspect.

Imagine a vast library with countless books. Each book represents a belief system, a doctrine, an ideology that we have inherited over generations. Some of these books are outdated, their contents no longer relevant, while others have been strategically placed there to control and dictate our thoughts. When we talk of conspiracy theories or the suppression of voices that challenge the status quo, it's akin to some of these books being labeled as "forbidden." Yet, the most curious among us will always peek, and in doing so, they might uncover truths that shake the very foundation of that library.

A helpful metaphor for our internal journey is that of a vast ocean. On the surface, the waves represent our fleeting desires and the chaos of daily life. Yet, as we dive deeper, the waters calm, and we start discovering the treasures within — our true values, our real aspirations, the essence of our being. Like the story of the prodigal son, we've ventured far, seeking external validation, but true solace is found when we return home, to the self.

As we embark on this introspective journey, the concept of minimalism takes on a profound meaning. It's not just about decluttering physical spaces but also mental and emotional ones. It's about quieting the noise, silencing the incessant demands of the ego, and tuning into the whispers of the soul. It's in this stillness that we discern what is fundamentally valuable.

For those who believe in life beyond our earthly existence or reincarnation, there's an understanding that material possessions are transient. The only true wealth we can take beyond this incarnation may be the wisdom we accrue, the lessons we learn, and the evolution of our character. These are the treasures that transcend lifetimes.

The spiritual path, though universal in its essence, is uniquely tailored for each traveler. It's a sacred journey, and its most profound moments are often deeply personal, meant to be cherished within, rather than showcased to the world. These experiences are not badges of honor but gentle reminders of our true nature.

As we evolve, our relationship with our planet undergoes a transformation. No longer do we see it as a mere chessboard on which we move our pieces, to win and dominate. Instead, we recognize it as an embodiment of beauty, a reflection of our inner state. Mother Earth is not a resource to be exploited but a living, breathing entity, mirroring our own vitality. When we harm her, we harm ourselves; when we nurture her, we heal ourselves.

In conclusion, as we journey from outer conquering to inner nurturing, we aren't merely transitioning from one activity to another. We're shifting paradigms. We're evolving from a race that conquers to a community that cherishes. This isn't just a change of action; it's a transformation of self. And as with any profound journey, it's filled with challenges and revelations, with moments of doubt and epiphanies. But through it all, there's the promise of arriving at a destination that's not marked on any map but is felt deeply within the heart.

VII.
THE "WE" COMMUNITY IS KEY

"We" in the inclusive meaning, not in an exclusive order, is a powerful key to unlocking our best future. "We" are not in this alone; in fact, everyone is in this crisis event together, regardless of their socioeconomic position in the world. Without money to insulate them, many of the urban elite are the most vulnerable. They often lack tangible survival skills and are dependent upon servants and employees. While some of the more impoverished people, who live in desolate and undeveloped areas on our planet, have very tangible survival skills and will be among the most resilient when coping with devastating impacts from the environment's loss of its "sweet spot" — the loss of the zone of homeostasis that life loves to inhabit.

There are some wealthy people who have invested in elaborate fall-out shelters; underground habitats with years of food and supplies in which they can hunker down during the anticipated chaos. I suspect this strategy may not work out as well for them as they might believe. I suggest security will best be created by working together to create new forms of villages that nurture the ways closer to the natural ways of living. The adage, "United we stand, divided we fall," isn't just an age-old saying or sentiment of unity; it's the tangible power of collective intent, a truth that echoes from the discovery of fire to the interwoven networks of the digital age.

While there may be special interest groups, moguls, or political systems that control the media and vast networks, who can put out "the spin" 24/7 — promoting propaganda, endeavoring to orchestrate narratives, such as the economy is more important than the ecology, or the crisis weather events are only natural cycles, or we just need to trust elected officials and the system and continue the way we've always been going. This type of rhetoric will fool fewer and fewer people. It cannot eclipse the truth nor stifle our shared heart-felt alliances. It will not replace the collective voice that resonates deeply within our hearts. The loudspeaker of squawking propaganda, reminiscent of dystopian futures and dark chapters of history, cannot drown out the harmonious melodies of a united people or dim the light of this growing torch of passion.

As we stand at a crossroads of change, facing challenges about to shake the very foundations of our planet, it is paramount to remember that "we" as a collective are the most powerful force in society, a symphony of synchronized hearts and minds. We are not a frenzied mob that will trample the opposition. As we plan together, aligned by our evolving values and shared vision, supported by AI, the internet, and other advancing technologies we will use harmoniously, we become a force of nature's intelligence and selective evolution. Our innermost knowing synchronizes as gyroscopes to stabilize our awareness and collective actions in the right direction to help us shape a new future. As we stand for the natural world, we know in our hearts this is our destiny. May we always remember: "We" is not just a word; it is all of us united. It is our most powerful foundation.

Community Integration

An integral cornerstone of the Spaceship Earth Ethic is the reimagining, evolving, and deep integration within local communities. Immersing ourselves in the localized fabric of our immediate surroundings isn't merely about fostering social bonds; it's about recognizing the collective strength and wisdom that emerges from people uniting with others in the local economy, as well as reuniting with the surrounding land and localized food production. By understanding and respecting the diverse tapestry of backgrounds, skills, and perspectives within our neighborhoods and towns, we can craft solutions that are both holistic and sustainable. By encouraging and supporting local organic and natural food production, we become healthier and more resilient to global breakdowns and supply shortages.

The act of community integration moves us from the abstract to the tangible. It allows us to witness firsthand the interconnectedness of our actions and the ripple effects they produce. The collective potential is multiplied when individuals come together for shared purposes. Rather than being a pebble cast into the collective ocean of the world economy, we take shape as an important component within the mechanism of our immediate community.

As we advance as collective caregivers, we will foster a deep sense of being a part of a vibrant, tangible, and often messy community that helps equip us with empathy, collaboration, and shared responsibility necessary to better tend to our world, society, each other, and ourselves. By actively participating in and contributing to our communities, our EQ (emotional intelligence quotient) is naturally expanded and becomes more pertinent. We help the community flourish, and it cultivates an environment for our own personal and collective growth. Incorporating community integration into our ethos reinforces the idea that while each of us may be just a single thread, together, we weave a resilient and vibrant social fabric, one that can sustain and nurture life in all its myriad forms.

Valuing All Life

True community compassion extends beyond just the human realm to all forms of life. The intricacies of this concept are vast, given our natural ecosystem, where energy is exchanged through consumption, be it by eating plants or animals. Yet, the heightened capabilities and understanding humans have achieved beckon us to evolve from hunter-gatherers into compassionate caregivers of our entire biosphere. By acknowledging the immense worth of our planet's rich biodiversity, we more deeply comprehend Earth's intricacies and our own significant evolution and conscientious expansion.

Our transition from external dominion onto a path of personal development is not merely a change in perspective or philosophy. It represents an evolutionary progression that recalibrates our symbiotic relationship with every life form. Calibrating our inner growth with supporting the vast myriad of life existing within our natural domain aligns our thinking with our core need to be nurtured.

Developing our humane character establishes and integrates our place as protectors and lovers of nature on a cellular level, helping us awaken to our god or goddess-like nature. Our innate, humane values pave the way for our harmonious journey aboard Spaceship Earth. It sets the stage for humanity's third act character arch in our historical drama, replete with redemption and resolution, owning our transition so that we become divine expressions of compassion, creating sustainability and abundance for every inhabitant — human or other. Our humane nature may be our most universally cherished quality.

Extraterrestrial Influence?

Some people actually believe that extraterrestrial influences have shaped human civilization and development. While this notion is far from scientifically proven, the rumors persist that an extraterrestrial alliance has shared advanced technology with humans, either directly through classified relationships or subtly through forms of inspiration among receptive people.

Those who subscribe to this perspective find it plausible that other advanced alien civilizations are monitoring Earth. They contend it's improbable that humans are entirely alone in the universe. While unconventional, this viewpoint proposes that humans may be destined for stewardship roles off-world.

Some of the adherents to these beliefs claim our treatment of planet Earth is a test of humanity's capacity to inhabit other worlds without destructive consumption, and we are undergoing some form of probationary period to determine if we can productively participate in this larger galactic society.

While this is not an accepted view for many people, it could help to expand the conversation and perspective of what may be at stake. In this view, humans must make an evolutionary leap towards balanced resource use and ecological harmony to warrant assistance from advanced extraterrestrials.

These ideas about extraterrestrial influences propose an expanded context for human development. They highlight that our environmental and societal decisions have consequences beyond just this planet. Neglect, apathy, and the resulting destruction of our home planet may forfeit the opportunity to participate in this larger society now only seen in science fiction. Even without evidence, these concepts reflect humankind's purpose and conduct from a cosmic perspective. They may effectively underscore the notion and value of wisdom in wielding our powers. How we treat our planet and societies shows our readiness for greater universal responsibilities. Our legacy shapes life on Earth and may influence opportunities beyond this world.

An Open Call to Participate

The urgency of our current situation leaves no room for complacency. We need action, and we need it now. But where does one start? Is there a haven, a place of unity, free from the shadows of the past models tainted with self-promotion or manipulative control?

Years ago, spurred by a shared vision, some of us embarked on a quest. We sought an enlightened community, an organization, a network as a place to join forces, and a beacon of hope where we could come together with other like-minded souls to effect meaningful change.

After an exhausting search, our journey, though filled with passion, proved fruitless. But then, as often happens in tales of old, the universe staged a dramatic scene to climax our sojourn and delivered our truth to us: "How can you expect to find this place when it is your job to create it?" This message resonated deeply within our souls, yet translating it into reality proved to be easier said than done. It has been an uphill task that has led us down many paths of cultural isolation and attempts at expression that often ended when our resources were completely depleted. It seems ironic, a tragedy of our times, that while exploitation often reaps lavish rewards, endeavors to heal our planet find scant monetary support. It seems monetary gain often requires "exploiting the opportunity," while healing operates from an entirely different matrix than exploitation and strums harmony on the strings deep in our hearts.

We're at a pivotal moment in history, and it is not just about reclaiming our planet; it's about rewriting our collective narrative, steering our future into vigilant hands that share a unified vision, joined in what is clearly the right direction to proceed. I know it, you know it, we all know it — *if* we can step beyond our self-interests and special interest affiliations. Only those anesthetized by intoxicants of excessive wealth or are clutching onto favored dole-outs or lost in forms of addiction cannot see the obvious truth that this is the moment of our massive planetary shift, the time for the human race to stop racing and find true direction.

Embracing a new ethic is only meaningful if translated into action. Here are four key steps to begin your journey now:

1. Slow down and review your possessions and consumption habits to look for ways to simplify and minimize your lifestyle. Focus on what is essential to your internal core value and nurture who you are and what you truly need.
2. Seek out like-minded individuals and start group conversations, enabling the development of your local supportive community. See where interests align and enjoy your expanded social network and context.
3. Research and engage in conversations to share knowledge about climate change initiatives, sustainability, and evolved social participation practices.
4. Participate with others and learn from/with them on CrewOfSpaceshipEarth.com and share your plans and ideas with WayBeyond.ai.

Start with small steps. Your actions can also inspire others to embark on this collective journey.

We are not just building a movement; we are settling into ourselves, finding our resolution to build a future where the focus has shifted from a largely unconscious consumer-based economy to a society built upon conscious contribution, compassion, and universal equity. We do not need New Age Pharaohs to lend us the means to make a difference, we need our clarity, our shared intention, and an individual willingness to stand for what we know is right! Are You to be One of the Ones Counted among the Shifting Axis Mundi of our Time and Space?

Where to Begin?

This is not just a book — it's an invitation. An invitation to participate actively in the societal and planetary transformation we so urgently need.

If you are like us and have not found that equitable place that fosters collaborative effort and shares the rewards of the efforts, then maybe you can also help create such a space. At Joyful Alchemists, we've conceptualized and are crafting a suite of platforms geared towards our shared aspiration to be gifted to those engaged in the movement. Does this mean we are providing the world with the solutions for this change? No, it does not. What it means is that we have made a diligent effort to bring focus into our collective awareness of what is needed. We are working to structure solutions and offer them up for development as collective spaces specifically designed to facilitate this evolution.

We offer these platforms as mechanisms, not so that we become the next wealthy tech moguls, but to enhance the wealth of our being through expression and the wealth of contributing. Does this mean we do not want to get monetarily rich from them if they take off? Yes, I intend that these will not be wealth accumulation mechanisms in the old model of money for myself or the team, that these will be a collectively owned and managed system of interconnected platforms dedicated to collective abundance under our evolved scale of values.

AI's Role in Managing Complexity

As our world becomes increasingly interconnected and multifaceted, we face unprecedented complexity in addressing global management and planning challenges. Diverse viewpoints, competing interests, and the sheer scale of analyzing global systems can overwhelm traditional approaches.

This is where AI holds a unique promise. Advanced machine learning algorithms excel at finding patterns and meaningful relationships within massive, messy datasets. By crunching vast volumes of information encompassing social media discussions, scientific publications, news reports, and quantitative data, AI can derive insights and connections that far exceed human capacity.

We will explore the power of collective decision-making, the utility of AI in managing complex systems, and the ways in which we can interface with existing institutions to promote change. To further the use of AI and other advanced modeling tools, the Joyful Alchemists is committed to developing a software platform, WayBeyond.ai, specifically for the purposes described in this book, as a planning tool for crew members in this new era.

While I believe I see much of the direction we must take, as well as many macro-level solutions from a high-altitude perspective, I know I cannot personally answer the myriad of questions required to execute all of the plans I suggest in this book. I know from experience the devil is in the details, but what does that mean? My experience as a team leader of projects in various industries and as a producer in Hollywood revealed there are always issues that are not fully flushed out and can loom up to threaten the success of a project. However, a good crew with clear direction can solve many challenges efficiently and grow from the experience. I have faith that here on Earth is already the Crew of Spaceship Earth, and we can answer the wide array of questions, find solutions, and manage what is required to have this transformation work, as long as we are not aligned to agendas for our selfish gains and against the common good that works for us all.

WayBeyond.ai - An Open Platform for Change

In response to our increasingly complex world and the demand for new AI-driven solutions to support collaborative approaches, Joyful Alchemists has taken on the creation of WayBeyond.ai as a tool to address many multifaceted global challenges. It is a powerful solution through which we can collect, log, acknowledge, synthesize, model, and offer back the reconciled collective knowledge, needs, and planning of the Crew of Spaceship Earth.

Envisioned by the group Joyful Alchemists, WayBeyond.ai is an open platform for people worldwide to contribute proposals that are integrated into dynamic models for the future. Rather than more static top-down planning by elected officials, ideas and strategies submitted by the Crew of Spaceship Earth will be organized into a 3D model of Earth, assimilating local and global inputs across domains like ecology, society, economy, and philosophy.

WayBeyond.ai Evolves via Grassroots Participation.

Advanced natural language processing allows WayBeyond's AI to contextually analyze varied proposals from diverse groups, from Indigenous tribes to urban youth activists. It rapidly reconciles perspectives by identifying shared values and shaping them into coherent, integrated plans. When ideas conflict, generative algorithms can propose creative compromises and solutions. This collective intelligence engine constantly refines the model with more input.

WayBeyond serves as a critical bridge between grassroots advocates and government institutions. The synthesized proposals and sentiments on the platform provide policymakers with a broad public perspective and innovative solutions. WayBeyond also enables collective citizen agendas and amplifies public voices.

A Grassroots Alternative

Rather than seeking funding from major technology firms, WayBeyond aims to grow organically from our team's efforts and contributions, small donations, and modest membership or subscription fees. This grassroots model will ensure the platform remains collectively owned for the public good rather than serving corporate interests. Its open, decentralized nature makes WayBeyond a project ordinary citizens can collectively rally around.

By merging human creativity with AI, WayBeyond brings integrated planning within reach. It transforms a cacophony of voices into a solution-focused choir resonating with our common values and aspirations. This collaborative platform empowers us to become architects of our collective destiny. The future is ours to envision and manifest together.

Bridging Grassroots and Government

WayBeyond can serve as a critical bridge between grassroots movements and government institutions. The synthesized proposals and sentiments on the platform provide policymakers with a broad perspective of public views and innovative solutions. WayBeyond also enables collective citizen agendas and amplifies public voices.

By merging human creativity with AI, WayBeyond brings integrated planning within reach. It synthesizes a cacophony of individual voices into a harmonized choir that resonates with our shared aspirations and vision. This collaborative platform will empower crew members to become architects of our collective destiny. The future is ours to envision and manifest together.

A Glimpse Into Our Platforms

These platforms are envisioned to work in unison, each fulfilling a pivotal role in promoting our shared vision.

CrewOfSpaceshipEarth.com: A purpose-driven social networking platform. Here, relationships, collaborations, and ideas are contributed, developed, credited to their originators, and evolved synergistically with the help of WayBeyond.ai.

WayBeyond.ai: This AI engine will assimilate the submissions, evolve the new and existing concepts, and integrate these into a global collective planning matrix that is envisioned as organized into an interactive 4-D map of the world.

Anthro-Regenerative Communities (ARC): A transformative model for holistic community living, integrating sustainability and equity. ARC offers a shared platform for individuals and groups to mold their futures collaboratively.

Nature's Blueprint: A non-profit dedicated to addressing the pressing environmental imbalances we face. It's rooted in the belief that the natural world holds answers to many of our challenges.

These platforms are intended to be collectively owned and progressively shaped by their members, rooted in the principles of shared intelligence, collaboration, and planning. Think of them as flourishing ecosystems where collaborative efforts give life and collective aspirations evolve into mutual actions.

A Course in Miracles explains that the world believes that to possess a thing, it must be kept. Salvation teaches otherwise. To give is how to recognize what you have received. (ACIM, W-159.1:5-8.) The historical laws of Earth are based upon the principle of win/lose - I have it, now it is yours, so I no longer have it; while the laws of heaven multiply as they are given and shared. It is clear that these ideas will become stronger and more potent as they are shared and furthered among a larger base and reinforced with supporting action. Then there will be more to go around, not less.

Even on a physical level, this principle holds true with our shared purpose — as we create a healthy earth and strong holistic society, we have more abundance to share for the benefit of all, not just a few. While the extremely wealthy may have fewer physical possessions and dominance, they will have greater internal peace and share in the overall sense of well-being and prosperity encompassing the world. Rather than claiming a slice of an ever-diminishing pie, we aspire to nurture a thriving, holistic world where abundance is shared and celebrated by all.

Together, these platforms aim to empower the Crew of Spaceship Earth, helping each of us realize our innate creative potential.

Managing Spaceship Earth: An Awakened Perspective

If our planet were a ship, it would be one without lifeboats. There's no escape from the challenges we've wrought; our only option is to navigate them together. As custodians of Spaceship Earth, our responsibilities extend beyond national borders and personal interests. Just as a ship's crew operates in harmony, ensuring the vessel's safety and the well-being of all onboard, we, too, must recognize our shared fate.

Our activation is twofold. First, it's the understanding that we are not passengers on this ship but its caregivers. Every choice of what we consume, how we vote, or how we relate to one another determines the course of our collective journey. Second, it's the realization that our individual well-being is intrinsically linked to the whole. When the seas are turbulent, no single cabin on the ship remains unaffected.

Embracing the "Spaceship Earth Ethic" is not just an intellectual exercise. It's a *call to action*, a call to live with intention, to value collaboration over competition, and to recognize that in the dance of life, every step matters. As we shift from a mindset of extraction to one of reciprocity, from indifference to compassion, we naturally will be called upon to help those earlier in their process of awakening to their own positions and expressions to contribute.

Responsible management, particularly in a global movement, requires a harmonious blend of ethical conduct, sustainable practices, and effective communication. Certainly, many members of Spaceship Earth are qualified to help manage and advance these evolutionary agendas. While it does contain elements found in traditional management theories, this approach takes a broader view by considering the wider impacts on society, the environment, and future generations.

1. Visionary Leadership

Responsible management begins at the helm. Leaders should be visionaries who not only foresee the broader implications of decisions but are also grounded in ethical and sustainable values.

- **Setting Clear Objectives:** A clear, shared vision provides direction. This vision should be in line with the movement's goals and the larger good of society and the environment.
- **Leading by Example:** Leaders should demonstrate, in their actions and decisions, a commitment to the values and principles they advocate.

2. Stakeholder Engagement

- **Identifying Key Stakeholders:** Recognize everyone affected by the movement, local communities, governments, NGOs, and more.
- **Regular Communication:** Engage with stakeholders frequently to gather feedback, understand their needs, and address concerns.

3. Sustainable Practices

- **Resource Management:** Ensure resources — financial, human, or natural — are used efficiently and sustainably.
- **Long-term Perspective:** Decisions should not just cater to short-term gains but should also consider long-term impacts and sustainability.

4. Inclusivity & Equity

- **Diverse Representation:** All sections of the population should be represented, especially marginalized groups. This ensures a diverse range of perspectives and ideas.
- **Equal Opportunity:** Ensure that opportunities within the movement, whether for leadership roles or project responsibilities, are made accessible to all based on merit and capability.

5. Transparent Operations

- **Open Communication:** Maintain channels that keep members and stakeholders informed about decisions, progress, and challenges.
- **Accountability:** Leaders and managers should be answerable for their actions and decisions. This includes having systems in place for reporting and addressing any lapses or misconduct.

6. Continuous Learning & Adaptability

- **Feedback Loops:** Establish systems to gather feedback from the ground and adjust strategies accordingly continuously.
- **Stay Updated:** Be aware of global trends, technological advancements, and research that can be harnessed to further the movement's goals.

7. Conflict Resolution

- **Mediation Channels:** With global movements, disagreements are inevitable. Having robust mediation and conflict resolution mechanisms is crucial.
- **Respectful Dialogue:** Encourage a culture where differences are discussed respectfully, and consensus is sought.

8. Collaboration & Partnership

- **Build Alliances:** Work with other organizations, governments, and entities that share similar goals to amplify the movement's impact.
- **Shared Platforms:** Use shared platforms for knowledge exchange, pooling resources, and collaborative initiatives.

9. Ethical Considerations

- **Guiding Principles:** Establish a set of ethical guidelines that every member is expected to uphold.
- **Regular Training:** Ensure members are periodically trained on these principles and understand their importance.

10. Monitoring and Evaluation

- **Set Benchmarks:** Define clear metrics for success and periodically assess the movement's performance against these benchmarks.
- **Iterative Approach:** If something isn't working, dare to revisit and modify strategies.

11. Team Leadership

- **Team Organization:** Every division and operation should be anchored by an experienced leader. This leader should serve as a reference point, offering guidance and support and ensuring team members know whom to turn to for help or advice.
- **Team Accountability:** Leadership isn't just about guiding, it's about taking responsibility. Team leaders and managers must be accountable for delivering on the team's commitments, both in terms of time and budget. This accountability extends not just to their individual work but also to the output of their entire department or division. With leadership comes an inherent responsibility to ensure tasks are executed efficiently and effectively.

Managing a global movement responsibly amongst a multi-billion world population is a multifaceted endeavor. It calls for a balance between visionary leadership and grassroots engagement using advanced technological tools, balancing using time-honored core principles and adapting to changing realities. Responsible management ensures that the movement not only achieves its goals but does so in a manner that is sustainable, equitable, and beneficial for all involved.

VIII.
ABCS OF IMPLEMENTING TRANSFORMATIVE SOLUTIONS

I have pondered potential remedies to the pressing challenges we face for decades, as I have witnessed them emerge and grow to the levels they are now. While seeking solutions, I have consistently recalled the solid wisdom passed down from Indigenous cultures who understood sustainability as an inner path of living harmoniously on this shared earth. Their teachings, distilled from centuries of balancing needs with nature's rhythms, can ground us amidst turbulence. I've also been guided by the lessons of village life, where necessity nurtures collective responsibility, frugal innovation, and circular economies that minimize waste. These proven models can inspire us. But we can't romanticize the past; we must steward change in the complex global age.

Our task is one of integrating, not just replicating, traditional principles into the realities of modern society. This calls for discernment, to embrace technologies mindfully, to recalibrate rather than dismantle economic systems. We must be judicious gardeners, planting seeds of change without uprooting the entire terrain. It will take many hands gently applying pressure and working together towards goals that seem to me to be quite obviously beneficial.

Buckminster Fuller's metaphor of society as a grand ship is fitting. He describes how even a slight turn of the *trim tab* on a rudder transforms the journey ahead. A wise captain charts direction not by decree but by consulting his crew. So, too, we must recognize our collective captaincy of this vessel called Earth. Within each of us lies a trim tab of influence to guide our shared course.

In this spirit, I offer not lofty academic solutions but shifts we can personally and collectively make to align our trajectory with equity and sustainability. Recalibrating society begins with the individual that combines into the collective until they produce a global change. Tiny ripples of awareness, once joined, become waves of transformation.

The fire of change starts not with a roar but with the tiniest spark within a willing heart. Let us tend the embers together. This is where our personal journey intertwines with the larger societal evolution, proving that change doesn't always start with a massive revolution but often with a single decision, a single person, you. The following suggestions are intended as kindling to ignite our collective activation.

A. Ecological Interventions: Healing the Earth

The ecological imbalance is so pressing that we will first look into these solutions. If we cannot quell this storm, we may be so occupied with trying to survive that there may not be a real opportunity to do the rest.

Ideally, sweeping top-down conservation mandates would be implemented immediately, but this is often politically challenging. An incremental approach can demonstrate efficacy and build public support. For instance, a proposal to phase out all single-use plastics nationally would likely face resistance. However, evidence from cities that banned certain single-use plastics shows a reduction in waste and consumer adaptability. By first implementing such bans at a municipal level and establishing successful precedents, national-level policy reform becomes more tenable

Top-down conservation policies and corporate sustainability initiatives would need to be coupled with decentralized, community-led projects tailored to local ecologies. Indigenous groups and environmental stewards should be at the forefront given their place-based wisdom. Promoting regenerative agriculture, agroforestry, eco-village models, and renewable energy co-ops can catalyze the transition. Individuals can make lifestyle changes to reduce waste and use platforms like WayBeyond.ai to contribute ideas and resources to larger ecological interventions.

Organizations like Project Drawdown are performing vital work by identifying and sharing information on solutions to reverse global warming. Their research compiles expert insights on practices across sectors — from renewable energy to sustainable transportation — that can collectively reduce emissions. While they may not provide detailed technical designs, Project Drawdown serves as an invaluable resource for solution-oriented climate action by documenting effective approaches. https://drawdown.org/

Their work, along with the contributions of other research groups, provides us with a toolbox of interventions we can begin scaling up immediately. Platforms like WayBeyond.ai can further democratize this knowledge, allowing individuals and communities to not only access these solutions but also collaborate on tailored implementations. By harnessing the power of information sharing and grassroots innovation, a multifaceted response can emerge.

Given the gravity of issues like climate change, biodiversity loss, and pollution, ecological restoration should be our foremost priority. Drastic action is needed to transition towards sustainability.

Under the guise of the threat of COVID-19, the world shut down most of the unnecessary travel, and as a result, the environment was given a temporary reprieve. Certainly, the environmental imbalance and crisis we are facing is far more serious than COVID-19 flu. Why can we not shut down non-essential parts of the economy to save our future from disaster?

Here are some suggestions to address urgent environmental actions:

Emergency Response Plan:

- Immediately halt any new fossil fuel projects and phase out existing ones rapidly but responsibly. Switch subsidies to support renewable energy projects, and allow for the production of free, non-polluting energy machines.

- Pass bold regulations to conserve forests and wilderness areas. Ban deforestation except for essential infrastructure projects.
- Institute a moratorium on deep-sea trawling and move towards sustainable fishing quotas informed by science.
- Finance the large-scale cleanup of waterways, plastic pollution, and derelict fishing gear in oceans. Mobilize volunteers.
- Enact ambitious carbon pricing and caps on emissions, prioritizing the most polluting industries. Level the playing field.
- Immediately halt the production of lethal poison chemicals that have more healthy ecological alternatives.

Rebalancing Our Footprint:

- Subsidize and support regenerative agriculture practices like crop rotation, composting, and integration of trees and plants.
- Subsidize and support regenerative grazing beef, livestock, poultry, and dairy products.
- Discontinue any subsidies and support for conventional agriculture, feedstock meat, and dairy providers.
- Remove non-essential paving and roads to reduce heat build-up and allow the ground to breathe, sequester carbon, and grow life again.
- Invest significantly in ecological restoration efforts for forests, wetlands, coral reefs, and other crucial ecosystems.
- Create more marine reserves, especially around sensitive habitats like seagrass meadows and mangroves.

- Subsidize and support sustainable transitions for fisheries, transportation, manufacturing, and energy sectors.
- Sharply reduce single-use plastics and pioneer closed-loop supply chains and circular economic policies.

Critical Enablers:

- Finance green initiatives through measures like carbon taxes, plastic taxes, and closing tax loopholes for polluters.
- Build partnerships between governments, businesses, communities, Indigenous groups, and environmental organizations.
- Leverage technology innovations around renewable energy, biodegradable materials, green chemistry, and precision agriculture.
- Empower and amplify the voices of youth climate activists demanding action and accountability from leaders.

Individual Action:

- Buy organic and regenerative agriculture, free-range poultry, grass-fed meat, and dairy products, and adopt a more plant-based diet.
- Use public transport, walk or cycle, and carpool, whenever possible. Reduce air travel.
- Support environmental organizations through donations, volunteering, or outreach. Get involved in local conservation.

- Vote for leaders who pledge urgent climate action and for policies advancing sustainability.
- Divest from fossil fuels and invest in renewable energy cooperatives and microgrids. Move savings to ethical banks.
- Join citizens assemblies demanding bolder action from governments and corporations to restore ecological balance.

With coordinated efforts across all levels of society, we can transition towards an economy and lifestyle centered around ecological balance, stewardship, and regeneration. What we need is the will and determination to act now before it's too late.

Philosophical Support:

- **Protecting Biodiversity:** Indigenous peoples have always protected biodiversity. We should do the same, safeguarding endangered species and conserving natural habitats.
- **Rehabilitating Degraded Areas:** There are plenty of areas that can be redeveloped for housing and other uses. Some of the worst dilapidated and run-down areas can be made better, even into the best.
- **Preserve Nature Areas.** There is no justification for developing even one more parcel of nature Zones. Some land areas should be returned to the other creators of Earth.
- **Restoring Ecosystems:** Like in Star Trek, we need to see ourselves as caregivers of our planet. Restoring damaged ecosystems, replanting forests, and cleaning up polluted areas should be among our top priorities.

- **Reversing Desertification:** In the last century, the total percentage of desert on the Earth has started increasing due to modern agricultural processes and climate change, having devastating effects upon the Ecology of the ecosystem and its ability to sequester carbon. Desert areas must be revitalized into grasslands for grazing and then can be replanted with trees as new areas of the desert are restored to fertility.

  Intensive agriculture has come at a steep cost of world soil loss. As an example, according to a recent study published in Earth's Future, over 57 billion metric tons of topsoil have eroded from farmland in the Midwest since farmers began tilling the prairies 160 years ago. This erosion has continued despite conservation efforts implemented after the 1930s Dust Bowl, with current rates estimated to be twice the level deemed sustainable by the U.S. Department of Agriculture.

  The study utilized high-resolution topographic surveys of native prairie remnants and surrounding cultivated fields across the Midwest. By comparing erosion levels at these borders, researchers found that soil thickness on hilltops has declined at an average rate of nearly 2 millimeters per year over the past century and a half. At this pace, future crop production could face severe constraints from depleted soils if erosion persists. The findings underscore both the alarming scale of topsoil loss from Midwestern agriculture as well as the urgent need to halt further erosion through regenerative practices.

- **Promoting Sustainable Living:** We should look towards traditional Indigenous practices of living sustainably with nature, such as permaculture, and combine these with futuristic technologies to reduce our ecological footprint.

  Permaculture techniques used in Indigenous agriculture, such as intercropping and agroforestry, can be synthesized with modern precision farming methods. For instance, sensor systems can map micro-climates and soil nutrition levels to determine optimal crop placements maximizing synergies, and integrating Indigenous wisdom and modern technology. While industrial agriculture must ultimately transition to regenerative models, incrementally blending techniques informed by tradition and science can ease this shift.

- **Human Biomass Project:** As humans become an ever-growing percentage of the Earth's total large animal population, we have a greater need and responsibility to replenish the earth's fertility to maintain the broader balance of the ecosystem. Biosolids or humanure are widely used as components in fertilizer. The main problem is that sewage sludge is loaded with heavy metals from various household cleaning products, or businesses, such as automotive and industrial shops. So in effect, we are spreading very toxic heavy metals into our food supply and cultivation environments. This is a solvable problem if we set the intention to fix it. While proposed solutions like effective biomass collection and redistribution without heavy metals seem unrealistic to some people, to others it is beyond question that it MUST be done if a large population is to survive into the future.

It is logical, obvious, and even our sacred duty to rejuvenate the earth's fertility using our own organic waste. By isolating our biological matter from nature's cycles, we risk an unsustainable depletion of planetary resources. Transmuting human by-products, such as feces, urine, and gray water, offers a chance to regenerate soil, recreate grazing lands, and potentially counteract desertification.

This encompasses not only utilizing our organic waste in sustainable ways but also ethically managing our population growth and recycling our discarded bodies. To treat our used discarded bodies in ways that disregard the cyclical return of our organic matter to nature, we're not honoring life's continuum but rather subscribing to a misguided ethos. This is our opportunity to tangibly reciprocate, transfiguring our waste into vital sustenance for our world. In this manner, every aspect of our existence, even those we often choose to overlook, can be harnessed to contribute to the cyclical and rejuvenating processes of nature.

While sweeping systemic changes are imperative, the collective shift begins at the individual level. Alongside large-scale ecological and economic interventions, each of us can integrate key personal strategies to align with the goals of balance, equity, and sustainability.

B. Personal Strategies to Support the Collective Shift

To facilitate a true paradigm shift, every individual must commit to personal transformation. By embodying strategies in alignment with the goals on a personal level, we can catalyze a collective movement toward a more harmonious and balanced future. Here are some strategies tailored for individuals:

1. **Mindful Consumption:** Each purchase we make sends a message. By supporting eco-friendly and ethically produced products, we vote with our wallets for a more sustainable and just economy.

2. **Continuous Learning:** The world is evolving rapidly, and continuous learning ensures we keep up. Engage with literature, seminars, or courses related to sustainable practices, Indigenous wisdom, or futuristic concepts.

3. **Mental and Emotional Well-being:** Practices like meditation, journaling, or engaging in therapy can help align our internal compass. Being emotionally balanced empowers us to make conscious choices and engage positively with the world.

4. **Engage in Community:** Whether it's a local neighborhood group, an online forum, or a global organization, being part of a community fosters a sense of belonging and shared purpose. This collective energy can be directed towards larger transformative initiatives.

5. **Practice Energy Efficiency:** Simple acts like turning off lights when not in use, using public transport, or recycling can significantly reduce our carbon footprint.

6. **Honor Ancestral Wisdom:** Take time to understand the Indigenous practices of your ancestors or local communities. These traditions often offer insights into sustainable living and a deep connection to the land.

7. **Digital Detox:** Periodically disconnecting from the digital world allows us to reconnect with nature, our communities, and ourselves. This practice cultivates mindfulness and reduces our digital carbon footprint.

8. **Grow a Green Thumb:** Whether it's a windowsill herb garden or a backyard vegetable plot, cultivating plants can teach patience, provide fresh produce, and foster a deeper connection to the Earth.

9. **Share Knowledge:** By talking to friends, family, and colleagues about sustainable and ethical practices, you amplify the message and inspire others.

10. **Personal Accountability:** Set tangible goals for your sustainable journey. Regularly review and recalibrate your path, ensuring you are continually evolving and growing in your commitment.

Remember, each individual's journey towards a more sustainable future will be unique. However, by integrating these personal strategies, we can do our part so that our collective efforts have a profound impact. It is also important to recognize that while individual choices are important, they exist within larger economic frameworks. Just as personal strategies help us realign from within, economic reforms can reshape the external landscape.

C. Economic Strategies for a Balanced Future

While the economic interventions we propose aim to fundamentally recalibrate our systems, it is crucial we balance transformative visions with evidence-based, incremental steps. For instance, one idea is a cap on excessive inheritance, but simply mandating this could meet intense political resistance.

The heart of an economy lies not in its bustling markets or soaring stock indices but in its ability to nurture the well-being of its people and the environment. Taking a cue from the Indigenous communities and the evolved society of Star Trek, here's a blueprint for an economically balanced future:

- **Equitable Resource Management:** Mirroring the post-scarcity economies like that of Star Trek, we need to harness our technological advancements to minimize wastage and to redirect resources so that everyone's fundamental needs are met. This would involve improving supply chain efficiencies, reducing food wastage, and enhancing global distribution networks.
- **Universal Participation:** Drawing from Indigenous societies that value every member, future economies should not just provide access to resources but should also empower each

individual to contribute their unique skills and knowledge. This involves creating platforms for skill-sharing, and vocational training, and encouraging localized proprietorship.

- **Nature-Centric Economic Activities:** Embracing the teachings of ancient communities, we should evolve our economy to coexist with nature rather than exploit it. Adopting agroecology, shifting to renewable energy sources, and promoting circular economies where waste is continually repurposed is pivotal.

- **Reimagining Inheritance:** Instead of perpetuating economic divides by passing down vast fortunes, there should be a cap on inheritance. The excess could fund community projects or be reinvested into the system to benefit all. This doesn't negate the value of legacy but reframes it to benefit the larger community, ensuring every generation works towards real-time societal advancement.

- **Green Production Mandate:** Manufacturers should be incentivized, and when necessary, mandated to redesign their production processes. This involves phasing out harmful substances, innovating eco-friendly alternatives, and actively restoring any environmental damage caused in the past. By holding industries accountable, we can usher in an era where every product made aligns with the principles of ecological balance.

- **Supporting Human Resources:** Economic policies should prioritize enabling individuals to pursue meaningful work aligned with their purpose rather than solely profit-driven jobs. Compensation should be based on the value created for communities rather than only financial return.

Alongside economic recalibration, innovations in our social fabric can foster the values of sustainability, equity, and human potential.

D. Social Innovations: Building Communities of Change

Research on successful community initiatives reveals that change is often most sustainable when led from the ground up. For example, studies of microfinance programs in East Africa show that locally-developed initiatives had higher participation and lower default rates than top-down government programs. Hence, while visionary, it may be prudent to first prototype concepts like education reform in smaller cooperative communities to demonstrate efficacy before advocating for national reform. Concrete success cases can bolster the pragmatic case for systemic change.

To bring about lasting change, it's crucial to embed it within our very social fabric. This requires inspiration from varied sources: the time-tested traditions of Indigenous communities, the unity-centric models of 19th-century village societies, and the advanced perspectives of futuristic visions such as Star Trek.

1. **Harmonious Cohabitation:** Indigenous tribes once flourished not merely because of their rich traditions but also because they inherently understood the value of living

harmoniously. By nurturing mutual respect, understanding, and shared responsibilities within our communities, we can recreate this harmonious cohabitation.

2. **Evolving Education:** Drawing from the futuristic world of Star Trek, where knowledge is highly prized, it's essential to prioritize lifelong education. This includes not only academic learning but also the preservation and sharing of traditional skills, ensuring every member of society is equipped with diverse knowledge.

3. **Mentorship and Guardianship:** Rooted in the age-old traditions of many cultures, the mentor-apprentice model is immensely powerful. By reintroducing this, we can ensure the transfer of knowledge, skills, and wisdom from one generation to the next, allowing each individual to stand on the shoulders of giants.

4. **Unlocking Potential:** Every individual is a reservoir of untapped potential. Taking a leaf from Star Trek's book, it's essential to cultivate an environment where everyone is encouraged to explore, nurture, and express their unique skills and passions.

5. **Rehabilitation and Integration:** Our society's strength lies in its ability to uplift and reintegrate its most vulnerable members. This includes those who've fallen between the cracks-addicts, the homeless, and others marginalized by societal structures. Drawing inspiration from both Indigenous communities and Star Trek's inclusive ethos, we must actively

work to provide these individuals with the resources, support, and opportunities they need to reclaim their lives and reintegrate into the community. Only by ensuring that every individual thrives can we truly say our society prospers.

E. Intelligent Food Production

Current industrial agriculture is a key driver of ecological decline. Toxic pesticides annihilate essential pollinators and soil microbes while polluting waterways. Heavy tilling and mono-crops degrade once-rich topsoil. Crammed factory farms (CAFOs) foster disease while generating massive waste streams. Industrial fishing decimates ocean life.

To nourish billions without destroying ecosystems, we urgently need an agricultural revolution.

Adopting Regenerative Agriculture:

Regenerative techniques like cover cropping, compost application, conservation tillage, crop rotation, and interplanting build soil health by emulating nature. Cover crops prevent erosion while their roots deposit carbon compounds. Compost enriches microbial life and water retention. No-till farming avoids soil disturbance. Crop rotation prevents pest buildup and nutrient depletion. Interplanting provides natural pest control. Overall, the aim is to end our war against nature in food production by proactively nourishing the soil-plant ecosystem.

Returning to Integrated Small Farms:

Industrial mono-crop operations, focused on economies of scale, should transition towards smaller integrated farms growing diverse crops and livestock. Animals naturally fertilize fields, while crop byproducts and food waste can feed livestock — closing the loop in a sustainable circular system. With animals and plants coexisting, farms can largely be self-contained ecosystems. Produce and meat can be sold locally, minimizing transport. Small farms also foster community and preserve agricultural knowledge.

Utilizing Biological Pest Control:

Chemical pesticides breed resistant superbugs yet annihilate pollinators and birds that naturally regulate pests. Biological controls via beneficial predatory insects, bacteria, and bird populations must be restored. Ladybugs, lacewings, bats, frogs, spiders, and select birds can keep pest populations in check if ecosystems are rebalanced after decades of chemicals. Some firms already offer natural pest control pairing records of pest levels with timely release of predators.

Transitioning to Pasture-Raised Livestock:

Factory farms confine animals in crowded, stressful conditions requiring huge antibiotic doses that impact human health. Shifting to grazing small herds across open pastures is gentler on animals and the land. Grass-fed livestock also provides healthier fats than grain-fed CAFO meat. Portable shelters and fencing allow herds to rotate, mimicking migrations that fertilize and enrich land. Managed grazing restores landscapes and prevents mega-fires. Integrating silvopasture

— combining trees, grazing, and forage plants — boosts biodiversity and carbon sequestration while producing food.

Thoughtful Permaculture Design:

Permaculture's design system leverages patterns in nature to maximize yields. Strategic zonation places frequently tended plants near homes while setting animals appropriately. Polycentric mandala garden plots intermix species to fill diverse needs in a compact space. Vertically layered forests with canopy, shrub, and groundcover plants increase total productivity. Thoughtful perennial plantings, cover crops, and natural water features reduce maintenance. Every element serves multiple functions, eliminating waste.

Building Sustainable Fisheries:

With demand outpacing populations, establishing marine reserves, regulating gear types, and banning destructive practices like dredging and driftnets are imperative. Bottom trawling scrapes up entire ecosystems — it must end. Expanding protected marine zones allows fish stocks to recover while supporting carbon-sequestering vegetation. To supplement sustainable wild-caught seafood, well-run recirculating aquaculture systems can grow select species efficiently with minimal pollution. Community-supported fisheries, cooperatives, and certificates for sustainably harvested seafood empower consumers and artisanal fishermen.

Localized Production and Distribution:

Long supply chains via fossil fuel-reliant trucks undermine food's sustainability. Bio-regional production where growing conditions are ideal cuts transport miles. Urban farms, vertical agriculture, neighborhood CSAs, edible landscaping, and community gardens boost local access to the freshest food. Farm-to-table programs connect regional hubs to consumers. Apps can allow home cooks or grocers to distribute surplus food rather than wasting it.

Promoting Plant-Forward Diets:

A global shift towards largely plant-based diets is critical to sustainably provide calories and protein. However, small amounts of meat, dairy, and eggs from pasture-raised animals can still have a place in moderation, while supporting ecosystems versus degrading them. Education programs can ease the cultural transition while promoting culinary traditions not centered on meat. Supporting humane working conditions for food systems laborers is also essential.

Leveraging Technology Responsibly:

From biointensive covered farming to AI optimization of inputs, technology can dramatically reduce ecological footprints. Hydroponics and aeroponics maximize yield in small spaces while minimizing water usage. GPS, Big Data, and AI can micromanage water, nutrients and other resources down to each plant. Gene editing may create more resilient crop varieties, but caution is needed to avoid uncontrolled effects. Any innovations must align with ecological principles and collective benefit.

Closing the Loop with Waste Streams:

Standard practices create linear waste pathways. But ecologically, there is no such thing as waste — every output can be an input for another process. Safely routing agricultural residues, food waste, livestock manure, and even human excreta back into food production closes the loop. Done properly, regenerative systems produce no net waste at all. Constant resource cycling replenishes soils and fertility.

By aligning food production with ecological wisdom, we can nourish ourselves while also restoring the planetary ecosystems we depend upon. This journey requires ending the extractive industrial food model and reawakening our symbiotic relationship with nature. When guided by permaculture principles and Indigenous insight, farmers become protectors of the living landscape. A regenerated food system can provide the basis for transforming all aspects of our economies into closed-loop sustainable paradigms where one entity's waste becomes another process's essential input.

F. Ecological Energy

Our modern existence is underpinned by tapping into the earth's reserves of fossilized sunlight. Ancient biomass converted into coal, oil, and gas provides over 80% of current energy, powering societies worldwide. But combusting these in a couple of centuries when they took millions of years to form is untenable. They're finite, and burning them floods the atmosphere with carbon that once was steadily sequestered underground. We are living far beyond our current energy means.

Continued reliance on fossil fuels will deplete these resources critical for future generations. Oil, as the most versatile hydrocarbons, may provide essential compounds for manufacturing and space exploration. Squandering it now on fuel jeopardizes potentials not yet envisioned.

Moreover, the pollution impacts from extracting and burning fossil fuels generate immense ecological harm. From Alaska to Ecuador, oil spills despoil habitats and threaten Indigenous cultures. Fracking earthquakes and flaring methane into the skies while communities nearby suffer health effects displays the industry's callous disregard.

Even supposedly "cleaner" fossil gas requires leaking pipelines stretching across fragile landscapes. The impact of mining and burning coal, the dirtiest fossil fuel, is an unquestionable driver of ecological catastrophe and climate chaos.

Nuclear power holds theoretical promise but has significant operational safety issues, radioactive waste byproducts lasting millennia, costs, and weapons proliferation risks are technologically unresolved. Hydroelectric impounds critical riparian habitats while hydrogen's widespread use could endanger stable water molecule structures.

The only truly sustainable path forward is renewable energy. Solar, wind, geothermal and marine power can be generated perpetually, including off-grid applications. Instead of global power distribution, decentralized and distributed renewable generation minimizes footprint while boosting community resilience.

Intelligently designed renewables present our greatest hope for an ecological energy future.

A potential limitation of large-scale renewable transition is the adequate availability of essential minerals like lithium and cobalt for technologies like batteries. As electric vehicle usage grows, lithium reserves are being rapidly depleted. By some estimates, economically viable lithium could be exhausted within decades at current rates.

This underscores the need for comprehensive recycling programs to recover lithium and other precious minerals from spent technology. Additionally, responsible and equitable lithium mining standards are essential for fair worker conditions and for preventing environmental harm. Research into alternative battery technologies not reliant on lithium also needs priority. Even abundant renewables like solar and wind require judicious use of essential finite resources.

We have the innovation to meet our needs while respecting planetary boundaries — but the corporate political will remains lacking. Hard as it may seem, even disruptive innovations like the mythical "Newman Motor" would have to contend with an entrenched energy-industrial complex wary of losing its firm grip over resources, grids, and metering.

Nonetheless, from policy reform to individual lifestyle choices, we must collectively transition towards renewables rapidly while curtailing energy consumption and waste. The goal should be maximizing efficiency to provide dignity for all, rather than permitting unchecked usage. With ethics guiding us, and technology as our ally, living sustainably within our planetary means can power our next epoch.

IX.
THE POWER & ROLE OF COMMUNITY

As I have journeyed along my path of personal transformation, I have become increasingly aware of the need for bridge structures between the sustainable ways of the past and our current depleting system. This is where community comes in. It has become increasingly evident that our current societal frameworks are not only unsustainable but also disconnected from the cyclical rhythms that support life. The challenges we face necessitate not just incremental changes, but a substantial reimagining of how we live and interact with each other and our planet.

For the past 15 years, I lived in Southern California within an intentional ecological organic farming community. First, I built my own house on their land with my own hands and little outside help. During my stay there I made a lot of soil, collected and composted food waste and coffee grounds from stores and restaurants in the area, and made most of the fertilizer needed for the gardens and orchards with the large worm bin I made to create organic worm tea. During this time, I grew tremendously due to my greater connection with the natural order of life and being connected to the soil and my own food production.

I have moved from the community, but not from my belief in the enormous value of communities. I am now in the process of writing a series of instructional books and building a consulting service called "ARC" Anthropological Regenerative Communities. I will hopefully create and be living back in an Intentional Community within a year or two.

ARC suggests that Intentional and Ecological communities offer a viable blueprint for our future society to move closer into harmony with the need to make these changes, offering a way to harmonize our existence with the natural world, promote social cohesion, and address economic disparities.

ARC: A Blueprint for Future Communities

ARC (Anthro-Regenerative Communities) The ARC model presents a blueprint for intentional communities. ARC is a pioneering initiative in collaboration with Joyful Alchemists at the intersection of real estate development, intentional communities, and sustainable living. Its business model is rooted in synergy with nature and promoting fulfilling relationships within the community. The ARC vision also promotes the resurgence of a modernized, yet holistic cyclical time, a concept that encourages us to reconnect with the Earth's natural rhythms. This shift towards cyclical living rekindles our bond with nature, grounds us in the tangible rhythm of the seasons, and nurtures a sense of unity within the community.

While the introduction of ARC in this book may seem to some to bear an element of self-promotion, it is vital to understand the ethos behind its creation. ARC is not just a concept; it's an open platform, a brainchild of Joyful Alchemists, envisioned as a global hub for collaborative thought and innovation. Rather than being an instrument for accumulating individual wealth, it's a dedicated space for collective ownership and operation within a non-profit framework. While it fully respects individual rights to property and equity, ARC's primary intelligence base and platform are designed to be transparent, accessible, and collectively owned.

Origins and Ethos of the ARC Model

The ARC model is the brainchild of John Schindler and Immanuel Solas, co-founders of ARC Enterprises, which was established in 2020. John brings three decades of experience in commercial and multi-family real estate and finance with CBRE as well as community development. Immanuel offers extensive expertise in software development and technology integration, e-publishing, course and content creation.

United by a shared passion for sustainability, community building, and exploring the frontiers of human consciousness, John and Immanuel envisioned a collaborative platform where people could live in harmony with each other and the natural environment. This vision manifested as the genesis of the ARC model.

At its core, ARC seeks to foster a way of life that nurtures the physical, social, psychological and spiritual wellbeing of inhabitants while also honoring ecological limits and planetary boundaries. The model envisions human settlements as diverse, resilient ecosystems that value equity, spur innovation, and empower inhabitants through shared ownership and collaborative governance.

Critically, the ARC model does not romanticize or advocate a return to primitive lifestyles. Rather, it thoughtfully integrates advanced technologies and sustainable design with the cooperative ethos and circular resource use of traditional communities. The aim is to create settlements that allow inhabitants to thrive while treading gently on Earth.

Recognizing the pressing need to address growing societal imbalances and the disconnect from the natural ways of life, I wrote *ARC: Anthro-Regenerative Communities — Sustainable Living Realized!* Along with ARC Enterprises, we offer a roadmap to create living spaces that embrace equity, sustainability, and interconnectedness. The ultimate goal of ARC is to create environments where forward-thinking individuals can come together, experiment, and create new, more harmonious models for community living that may proliferate into broader society.

The ARC model is a proactive response to social and economic disparities that exacerbate our current challenges. It proposes a lifestyle that fosters harmony with our planet while simultaneously promoting a sense of community and mutual support among its members. Importantly, ARC goes beyond merely advocating for change; it provides a viable blueprint for realizing a sustainable, equitable, and interconnected existence.

Key Features of the ARC Model

The ARC model comprises various interconnected elements and design principles:

- Mixed-use developments that integrate residential, agricultural, commercial, and green recreational spaces to promote sustainability and self-sufficiency.
- Extensive green infrastructure including rooftop solar panels, greywater recycling systems, community gardens/small urban farms, edible landscaping, and ecological waste management.
- Home ownership for members provides them stability and incentive for joining in the village long-term, potentially for generations.
- Shared community assets and resources to improve access and affordability while reducing environmental impact. These include shared gardens, water treatment and power plants, laundries, workshops, car-share/bike-share systems, and recreational facilities.
- Diverse, inclusive, and multigenerational communities that provide enhanced social connections and support systems.
- Robust digital connectivity using mesh networks, serverless architecture, and edge computing to enable efficient resource-sharing and collaboration.

- Innovative construction techniques utilizing locally sourced, non-toxic materials aligned with green building standards and circular economy principles.
- Shared ownership and equity structures of communal areas based on non-speculative community land trusts and housing cooperatives to prevent gentrification and displacement.
- Participatory governance models that empower inhabitants through inclusive and consensus-based decision-making on matters of community interest.
- Non-hierarchical organizational formats based on *sociocracy* and *holacracy* methodologies that distribute authority across self-organizing circles.
- Integrative health and wellness programs ranging from community acupuncture to biodynamic gardening, embodying a preventative and holistic approach to well-being.
- Lifelong learning opportunities through skills-sharing, mentorship programs, and community knowledge exchanges on topics like permaculture, green technology, parenting, etc.
- Economic structures focused on nurturing community-based microenterprises, collaborative ventures, sharing economies, and regional import substitution.

The ARC model is not a fanciful dream, but a comprehensive guide to establishing resilient, sustainable, and equitable communities. It recognizes the pressing need for societal change and affirms our capacity for collective transformation. In the tumultuous period we currently navigate, ARC can serve as a beacon of hope, illuminating the path towards a future where humans live in harmony with each other and the Earth.

ARC Model's Key Principles

- **Ecological Integration & Regeneration:** ARC communities deeply respect the environment, acknowledging the inextricable links between human survival and the health of our planet. These communities are designed to function in harmony with nature, from the use of renewable energy sources to the adoption of regenerative agriculture practices. This integral approach ensures that the ecological balance is maintained, preserving biodiversity, and allowing the Earth's resources to replenish.

- **Social Connection & Community Building:** In an increasingly fragmented world, ARC aims to restore our fundamental human need for connection. Each community is designed to foster strong, meaningful relationships, encouraging collaboration and mutual support. These connections are reinforced through shared responsibilities, community events, and the mutual pursuit of common goals.

- **Addressing Wealth Disparity & Home Ownership:** The ARC model is deeply cognizant of the social and economic imbalances that fuel our current crises. In response, it promotes equitable wealth distribution and aims to democratize access to housing. By providing avenues for affordable homeownership and fostering cooperative economic models, ARC seeks to reduce wealth disparity and cultivate financial resilience at the community level.

- **Revitalizing Cyclical Time Patterns:** A fundamental aspect of ARC is the shift from a linear to a cyclical perspective of time. This paradigm shift allows communities to align their rhythms with nature, fostering a lifestyle that is synchronized with the seasons, lunar cycles, and other natural phenomena. This harmony with cyclical patterns encourages a slower, more conscious lifestyle, fostering well-being, and reducing the stress associated with the relentless pace of modern life.

The ARC model, therefore, is not merely some utopian vision; it is a comprehensive roadmap and framework for planning, building, and fostering resilient, sustainable, and equitable communities. It acknowledges the gravity of our current predicament but also affirms the potential for collective transformation. As we navigate this tumultuous period, ARC may serve as a guide towards creating community models and villages where humans can evolve new models to live in harmony with each other and our Earth. Like ripples spreading across a lake, engagement within communities can spread visions of change far and wide.

The Anthropic Regenerative Community model represents one such boundary-expanding dream manifested. It ignites our creativity, intuition, and innovation to conjure into existence human settlements that epitomize sustainability, inclusion, and social synergy.

Spaces that provide not just shelter, but also nourish our deeper human yearning for meaning, purpose, and connection. Places where individuals can thrive without depriving others, where humanity and nature can flourish in symbiotic unity.

Settlements that heal, restore, and regenerate, transform our relationship with the planet and with one another. If there was ever a time for courageous dreaming, it is now. The possibilities are limited only by the scope of our collaborative imagination. The ARC model is one gateway into this enchanted realm of regenerative possibilities.

The challenges we face during this pivotal juncture of human civilization and planetary evolution call for radical imagination and courage. We must dare to dream of possibilities that transcend the boundaries of the status quo.

Transforming Struggle into Transformation

The deepest transformations often start with transcending, rather than mastering our own shortsighted impulses, regardless of the form they take. I have found that limiting or misleading impulses can take many forms and hide in plain sight, often in the guise of what we treasure. It is not uncommon that we can become threatened and defend the very things that we would best be served by letting go. Transcending these impulses often requires us to also question their very nature. Why do we feel threatened when asked to let go of something? Is it really that valuable, or have we been tricked by our minds into believing its importance? Like deciphering a complex illusion, we must shift our perspective to see things as they truly are, rather than how we fear they might be.

This insight lays the groundwork for what can be some of the most profound transformations in our lives. It allows us to be fully present, and to make choices based on our truest selves rather than reacting out of fear or misplaced attachment. And in that newfound clarity, we can navigate the world not as prisoners to our impulses, but as liberated individuals ready to grow and explore. Only then do we transcend the limitations of our immediate wants, needs, or fears, and allow our lives to blossom in directions we could never have foreseen.

This struggle is eloquently captured in the Bhagavad Gita, where Krishna likens taming the senses to harnessing wild horses. It is stated that the most difficult beast in the world to tame is our mouth, what we put into it, and what comes out of it. Just as horses must be either won over through a direct connection or broken before becoming useful, we, too, must engage our higher reasoning to overcome our addiction to sense stimulation and our innate compulsions if we are to be able to create a society that can endure and evolve.

If we do not find a way to composite, a balance between our hearts, minds, and actions, then inevitably, one way or another, a correction will be imposed upon us by some catastrophic means, be it by nature, war, plague or other means. The equation is simple math. Fortunately, there are many spiritual paths that assist people in this struggle. It is said that as each person attains any level of personal evolution and finds their peaceful center, it creates an expansive ripple effect that elevates the overall collective consciousness and this energy makes it easier for others to also come into balance. While it is not the purpose of this book to suggest any particular spiritual or religious path to help the readers polish the gems within, I do recommend that whatever means you find, you earnestly embrace the benefits and growth inherent within them.

To steer humanity towards sustainability, we must rein in these mad horses between our genitals and minds, and bridle our personal ambitions in favor of collective well-being. We can transcend our egocentric quest for dominance, and nurture the courage to focus on renewal, to redefine ourselves as caregivers of our planetary home. This involves a profound shift, from exploiting nature to healing it, from consuming endlessly to living purposefully. A transition is well underway and the time is now to align with the greater good.

Overriding our conditioned primitive drives for immediate pleasure and excess is a shift many people believe we are incapable of making. It is my contention that the qualities required for this transition to succeed are inherent within us, buried under layers of external conditioning that accumulated as a result of living with the previous harsh conditions of this world. These habits no longer serve us, and we will outgrow them. I am convinced that if we do not become steadfast in making this shift now, we will likely be forced to change, or many will perish. This massive wave of events that will force these changes may be coming sooner than many foresee.

No doubt this transition will be turbulent at times, much like breaking an unruly horse. But by channeling our collective will, intelligence, and compassion, we can transform individual urges into an ethos centered around balance, renewal, and harmony with all life. This is the next stage of our social and personal evolution, the emergence of a conscious species acting not on impulse but with wisdom. It starts by overcoming the mad horses of our senses, slowing down, and centering into what is really important so we are not racing in the wrong direction, but contributing our best to manifest our higher destiny. In other words, truly being yourself!

The Axiom of Capability Meeting Challenges

As we conclude our deep dive into the challenges and pitfalls of our current societal structures, we're left with a crucial understanding: our present trajectory is unsustainable. Yet, this realization is not a signal for despair but a call for innovation and learning. It's time to steer our Spaceship Earth in a new direction. To chart this new course, we will draw inspiration from the wisdom of our past and channel it into crafting a resilient and harmonious future. In the next section, we excavate valuable lessons from Indigenous practices, replicate the sustainability of the village model, and envision a future where growth is balanced and inclusive.

It's essential to recognize that challenges aren't only barriers but also opportunities. During these tests emerge a profound, almost metaphysical principle: challenges don't arise in a vacuum. They manifest when we, as beings of immense potential, have cultivated the strength and wisdom to address them. Embracing challenges accentuates our collective strength in overcoming them. It's as if the universe, in its infinite wisdom, knows that growth and evolution are born from adversity and ensures that challenges appear at the doorstep of capability.

Today, as we confront the cancerous tendrils of unchecked capitalism and entrenched power structures, as well as our challenge to bridal unhealthy impulses, it's essential to remember this axiom. These challenges have not arisen to defeat us but to push us to evolve. They beckon us to muster all of our collective knowledge, innovation, and spirit to craft a future we want our descendants to live in. We're not here by accident, or bystanders in this cosmic play, but active participants, chosen by time and circumstance to transcend our obsolete conditioning and the authoritarian power regimes that have long overshadowed humanity's true potential.

It may seem a monumental task, considering the depth of conditioning and the vastness and complexity of the systems we will modify. Yet, this is precisely the moment we've been preparing for, consciously or not. Every historical struggle, every innovation, every moment of unity in our shared history has been leading us to this pivotal juncture. The challenges we face are but reflections of our accumulated strength as a species, urging us to recognize our latent power and with courage and conviction lay down the tracks for the next leg of our journey.

In essence, these societal challenges are not mere roadblocks but rites of passage, marking our readiness to ascend to greater heights. It's not just about dismantling old systems but forging a new chapter in our collective story. And as we stand on the precipice of this new dawn, let's remember that the universe doesn't set tests it knows we can't pass. The very existence of these challenges signifies our readiness to evolve beyond them, ushering in an era where equity, sustainability, and shared prosperity are not ideals but realities.

We Can Make This Happen

We have the right and the power to evolve our society in the direction we collectively elect. Certainly, it is spelled out in the American Constitution and the voting structures within democratic countries. History bears witness to this type of collective action's power. Across the eons, the indomitable spirit of humanity has faced countless adversities. And time and time again, we've emerged, not defeated, but stronger and more unified. Deep within us lies an unwavering belief — the belief in our collective power to reshape the world. From monumental movements like civil rights to environmental advocacies, when individuals unite for a shared cause, transformative change becomes not just possible but inevitable. The narrative can shift, paradigms can alter, and together, we can rewrite the destiny of generations.

Today, as we stand at a crossroads, facing the colossal challenge of redefining our societal structures and values into a world that mirrors our shared aspirations, dreams, and the values we hold dear, let's remember our legacy. History doesn't merely recount events; it's a testament to our collective will. From the Earliest days of human civilization when tribes banded together to carve out homes from dense wilderness, through the evolution of many civilizations facing crisis, the Civil Rights Movement, the fight for environmental justice, the countless moments when ordinary individuals rallied together for extraordinary change — these aren't just footnotes in history books. They are blazing beacons, reminders of what we're capable of when we come together with purpose and passion.

Now, more than ever, we need to harness this power. We're not merely fighting against something; we are forging ahead for a brighter, more equitable, and sustainable future. And to those who may doubt or waver in the face of these daunting challenges, I say this: look around. Look at the person next to you, behind you, across from you. Realize that all around you lies a reservoir of potential, waiting to be tapped. The power isn't just in numbers but in unity, in the collective heartbeat that echoes the same dream. Is there not an underlying sense that we're here for something greater than what we've seen so far? As Paul McCartney so eloquently wrote in the song Blackbird, "Take these broken wings and learn to fly. All your life, you were only waiting for this moment to arise."

The narrative of our world is not set in stone. It's written each and every day by people just like you and me. We have the pen, the ink of our convictions, and the page of our actions. We don't just have the right; we have the responsibility, the power, and the means to steer our society in the direction that reflects our collective vision. Change isn't just on the horizon — it's here, within our grasp.

Together, as architects of our fate, it is our current job to rewrite the destiny of generations to come. So, as we cross-examine our narrative of the challenges and solutions along this journey, remember this singular truth: we've faced the odds before and triumphed. And even if we fall short of unwavering resolve and unity, we are still able to do it again. We CAN and WILL make this happen NOW!

In my spiritual beliefs, I envision an existence beyond our earthly realm where consciousness continues its journey.

I believe this life is an extension of our souls, created, in part, for the purpose of invoking our learning and ensuring our evolution. We are being prepared for yet another, even more expansive journey on a never-ending path. We travel along an intricate and infinite carpet woven of light from the trails left by the movements of celestial and terrestrial bodies since the dawn of time. This eternal tapestry records the story of all of life, woven by our collective experiences and interactions of all living beings everywhere and throughout all time. Our deep purpose entices us to participate in the creation of a divine playground for souls. Our physical forms serve the development while incarnate as the physical weaving instruments and foundation builders of this eternal time-space reality.

I understand myself to be a form of Gnostic — an individual with an intuitive sense of insight that allows me to perceive nuances of reality beyond the immediate and apparent. This direct intuitive perception serves as a tool for gaining a more expanded understanding of our greater multi-dimensional world. It often comes accompanied by an elevated awareness and sensitivity towards the physical and intellectual world, helping perceive subtle cues and patterns that may elude those engulfed deeper in the material realm and the pursuit of wealth. Some might define this process as gnosis — a deep spiritual knowledge derived from direct experience and insight rather than study or lineage of teaching. Can you resonate with this notion? My inner senses have frequently shown me facets of a more alternate reality, which I then seek to validate in the physical or intellectual world, often finding affirmation in sets of three validations.

Why choose to reveal this now, in this book? Do I seek to discredit my own work? No, I am actually seeking to connect with my audience. Undeniably, this disclosure may invite skepticism and criticism from some quarters, potentially undermining the perceived validity of this work. However, I sense a deeper truth in our collective consciousness, an undercurrent beneath the frantic pace of our reality, may be coming from our soul. I seek that connection with a part of you that, I believe, will resonate with the truth in my self-revelation. A part of you that may already be cognizant of the truth in these words, awoken or ready to awaken, to bloom, to believe in and express the limitless potential we possess, and to join as an active participant aboard our collective journey on Spaceship Earth.

Resuming our exploration of the concept of "remembering," in this context, implies the reattachment or reintegration of seemingly lost parts of our greater selves. It's about calling back the pieces of ourselves we may not even realize we have misplaced until we initiate and experience a *re-call*. We aim to re-call, re-member, and reattach parts of ourselves that reside beyond the periphery of what our physical senses can perceive. It is my belief that we may retrieve parts of ourselves that may be hidden, neglected, or forgotten in the recesses of our consciousness, including soul fragments that we may not even recognize until we intentionally call them forth, to rediscover a sense of and relationship with greatness that may be obscure in our culture, even in myth, yet remains ever relevant to our true selves and therefore our present reality.

Drawing upon wisdom from *A Course in Miracles*, we might contemplate the possibility that our greatest selves exist as God created us, perfect and whole. Yet, in our human experience, we may be dimensions away from the optimum version of our original selves. Maybe this disconnection is not because we have fallen from grace, but maybe because we have entered into a long trek, a sort of mission into the density of matter to add additional dimensions of density into the dream of creation — a program that we cannot recall consciously while in our temporary incorporeal limited form.

Could this be a reason why we often feel fragmented, disconnected from any sense of inherent greatness, seemingly lost in the annals of time and the confusion of material reality? Through the process of aligning with our divine essence, we may remember and recall our deeply embedded abilities and purpose, our innate potential.

As we bridge the divide between our present selves, grappling with formidable challenges, and our highest, truest potentials, we may discover the capability to overcome every obstacle encountered during this transition. It marks not just a beginning but the start of something far greater than words can express.

Part 3
Activating Our Destiny

You hold the key to our destiny

Stay true to your spirit, let wisdom guide
And have faith that providence is on our side
If we walk this destined trail with heart and might
We'll activate the promise of our shared light

X.
REDISCOVERING & REINTEGRATING OUR SELF

Just as our societal solutions require both inner and outer change, my personal journey demanded an integration of our external and inner worlds. At its best, I consider this life to be a dance between the spirit and the flesh. We move in a deep romance between our awakening intelligence discovering through our senses and tapping into the deep mystical pool of our innate BEing that we sometimes refer to as the soul, and other terms. Are we mortal, immortal, or both? It is cleat that our bodies wear out and do not last very long. The deeper question includes: Are we a result of our bodies? *or...* Are our bodies a result of us?

We have looked into some of the main challenges we face as a society and some of the potential remedies, we have journeyed a bit inward, shifting our focus from the outer world to the intricate dimensions of our inner selves. If you take a good look at the equation of where the power is, there is little doubt that the material plane is largely controlled by the dark ego which is largely short-sighted — it holds the guns, the bombs, and creates fear which it uses to control many of the structures that contain our society. If it were not for what I've experienced on a spiritual realm, the tug of war would certainly seem pretty hopeless. However, I am not without hope, nor is my hope blind. I'm filled with confidence because maybe I have seen beyond the veil of Pleasantville?

I've been asked whether delving into these spiritual and esoteric realms in a book primarily aimed at being pragmatic and practical might make me seem foolish. The unequivocal answer is yes, it might indeed appear that way, and perhaps being perceived as somewhat humorous is acceptable. After all, the notion that I (or *you*) can genuinely bring about change might also be viewed as a joke.

However, these last sections of the book are actually the parts that I look most forward to sharing. It is the essence of who I really am, and I believe it is who/what we really are, and who/what we are connected to that can act as an effective counterbalance to the external exploitation, obstructions, and societal constructs we've confronted thus far. The ideas I will share are not just fluff, but are also becoming recognized in science and psychology.

Bridging the realms of spiritualism, intuition, paranormal human powers, and quantum physics is a complex and evolving field, and it often involves exploring the interface between consciousness and the physical universe. Here are some key points and examples that showcase the connection between these areas:

> **Quantum Entanglement and Non-Locality:** In quantum physics, there's a phenomenon called entanglement, where two particles become connected in such a way that the state of

one instantly influences the state of the other, regardless of the distance separating them. This has led some to suggest a connection between the nonlocality of quantum particles and the idea of interconnected consciousness in spiritual and paranormal contexts.

- o Example: Research by physicist Alain Aspect in the 1980s confirmed the existence of quantum entanglement experimentally. This has sparked discussions about the implications of non-locality for human consciousness and interconnectedness.

Observer Effect: In quantum physics, the observer effect suggests that the act of observation can influence the behavior of subatomic particles. This concept has parallels with the idea that human intention and consciousness can affect external reality.

- o Example: Experiments in consciousness studies, such as those conducted by Dean Radin, have explored the influence of human consciousness on random number generators (RNGs), showing statistically significant deviations from chance, implying a connection between consciousness and the physical world.

Parapsychology Research: Parapsychology is the scientific study of paranormal phenomena, including telepathy, precognition, and psychokinesis (mind over matter). Some parapsychological research explores the connection between these phenomena and the quantum realm.

- Example: The Global Consciousness Project, initiated by physicist Roger Nelson, collects data from random number generators worldwide during significant global events. Researchers have reported correlations between deviations from randomness in the data and major world events, suggesting a possible link between global consciousness and quantum processes.

Intuition and Quantum Decision Making: Some theories propose that human intuition may be connected to quantum processes in the brain. The idea is that the brain could harness quantum effects to make rapid decisions or access information beyond what's available through classical neural processes.

- Example: Physicist Henry Stapp has suggested that quantum Zeno effect (the idea that repeated measurements can freeze an evolving quantum state) could be connected to the sense of knowing when making intuitive decisions.

Holistic Health and Quantum Biology: Emerging fields like quantum biology explore how quantum phenomena might operate in biological systems. This includes the idea that consciousness and intention could influence health and healing.

- Example: Some proponents of holistic health practices suggest that techniques like meditation and energy healing operate through quantum principles, influencing cellular processes.

Theoretical Physics: Theoretical physicists like David Bohm and Amit Goswami have explored the relationship between quantum physics and consciousness. They've proposed models in which consciousness plays an integral role in the universe.

While these connections are intriguing, it's important to note that these ideas are still in the realm of hypothesis and theoretical exploration. The intersection of spirituality, intuition, paranormal abilities, and quantum physics remains an area of active research and debate, and many scientists are cautious about making direct claims regarding these connections due to the complexity of both quantum physics and consciousness studies.

In the mystical and esoteric realms of spiritualism, which underlies almost all religions, a person's ego is so inflated that they cannot see what is right in front of them. If one cannot find humor or humility in the face of the divine or the mysteries of existence, then they are missing the point. Spirit often encourages a sense of playfulness, spontaneity, and not taking oneself too seriously. This is because the ego is rigid and its intellectual framework can be a barrier to perceiving the deeper truths of existence.

In spiritual wisdom across various traditions, there are many passages that reflect the idea that spirit discerns what the eyes cannot see. It is a common thread emphasizing the need to transcend the limitations of the ego or individual self to attain deeper understanding. This wisdom teaches that the divine or the mysteries of existence often elude those with inflated egos. Humility and humor in the face of the divine are seen as important qualities. Additionally, spiritual insight is believed to come not just from what the eyes perceive but from a deeper, intuitive level of awareness.

Here are some quotes and passages that reflect these themes:

From Taoism (*Tao Te Ching* by Laozi):

"*The Tao that can be told is not the eternal Tao; the name that can be named is not the eternal name.*" — This opening line from the Tao Te Ching highlights the ineffable nature of the Tao, suggesting that it cannot be fully expressed in words or concepts.

> "*He who knows, does not speak. He who speaks does not know.*" — This passage underscores the idea that true wisdom often resides in silence and direct experience, not in intellectual discourse.

From Buddhism (*Dhammapada*, a collection of sayings of the Buddha):

> "*The fool who knows he is a fool is that much wiser. The fool who thinks he is wise is a fool indeed.*" — This quote emphasizes the importance of humility and self-awareness in the pursuit of wisdom.

> "*Do not dwell in the past, do not dream of the future, concentrate the mind on the present moment.*" — This teaching encourages individuals to let go of attachments to ego-driven thoughts about the past and future and instead focus on the present moment.

"*The truth you believe and cling to makes you unavailable to hear anything new.*" — This quote underscores the idea that rigid attachment to beliefs and ego-driven views can obstruct true understanding.

These quotes capture the essence of the themes we're exploring, emphasizing humility, the limitations of the ego, and the importance of direct experience and present-moment awareness in the pursuit of deeper understanding.

In this next segment of our exploration, we will embark, hopefully with a sense of humor and humility, on a journey of "Reconnecting the Pieces: Remembering Ourselves."

This juncture, however, presents me with an intriguing quandary. How can I authentically guide you through my deep convictions and perspectives while laying bare some of my own relevant truths and beliefs without risking looking like a fool? I can't, so, I will deviate considerably from established models of science and human history — constructs often staunchly defended by traditional academia and societal power structures. If you have doubt, or a gasp of disbelief, just follow it up with a chuckle! Even so, the mainstream narratives of our origins, the nature of our existence, and our purpose, in my view, often fall short of encapsulating the profound magnificence of the human spirit we are when in sync with the cosmic symphony.

Recalling Our Latent Capabilities

The concept of latent genetic potential and untapped intellectual capacity is both tantalizing and complex. It resonates with the widely circulated but scientifically debunked myth that humans use less than 10% of their brains. More accurately, based upon measuring and mapping sections of the brain and measuring activity, it turns out that we use virtually every part of the brain. This does not mean however that we have nearly developed, discovered, engaged, or are utilizing the majority of our capabilities. Despite this misconception, it's true that we have huge potential for increasing our mental and genetic potential to its fullest extent. There are many examples of extraordinary capabilities by people in history and alive on Earth today. Maybe they are not the exceptions but the forerunners of who we are to become.

This opens an exciting avenue of exploration-unveiling our hidden capabilities and accessing the extraordinary potential that may lie dormant within us.

> Exploring our Genetic Potential: Our genetic code is incredibly sophisticated and intricate, containing approximately 20,000-25,000 protein-coding genes. However, our understanding of human genetics is still evolving. While we have decoded much of the human genome, we have yet to fully grasp how all of these pieces interact and what potential they may hold. The study of epigenetics - how environment and behavior can change the

way our genes are expressed - offers a glimpse into how our genetic potential can be activated. Factors like stress, nutrition, or exposure to toxins can turn certain genes on or off, influencing our health and behavior. As we continue to uncover the complexities of the genome, we inch closer to unlocking our full genetic capabilities. Careful scientific study paired with ethical consideration of application will be key as we seek to harness the tremendous possibilities within our DNA in the years to come.

Unleashing our Cognitive Abilities: When it comes to cognitive potential, it's more a question of optimizing the use of our brain's capabilities than discovering unused portions of the brain. Our brain is a dynamic organ, constantly rewiring and adapting itself. Practices like meditation, mindfulness, and cognitive training can help enhance focus, memory, and creativity, leveraging the brain's neuroplasticity ability to reorganize and form new neural connections. Certain techniques and technologies, such as neurofeedback and brain-computer interfaces, may also enable us to harness more of our cognitive potential.

Activating Human Potential: Stories of individuals accessing seemingly superhuman abilities during extreme situations suggest that we might possess latent capacities. For example, there are anecdotal accounts of 'hysterical strength', such as people lifting cars to free trapped individuals during emergencies. While the scientific basis of such phenomena isn't fully understood, they indicate the potential for extraordinary physical and mental feats under certain conditions.

The Frontier of Human Abilities: If we consider our genetic and cognitive potential together, the possibilities are staggering. It's conceivable that through a combination of mental training, lifestyle modifications, technological innovation, and a deeper understanding of our genome, we could unlock skills and abilities that are currently the stuff of science fiction-enhanced memory recall, heightened sensory perception, increased empathy, or even abilities we have yet to imagine.

While the prospect of activating our latent capabilities is undoubtedly exciting, it's important to view this not as a forced goal, but as a natural unfolding. The journey of awakening dormant abilities such as kundalini energy or elevating one's chakras can sometimes trigger overwhelming energy that may be challenging to navigate. Instead of pursuing these outcomes aggressively, we invite you on a path where the transformation happens organically through an attuned understanding and expression of your unique needs and potentials.

Please note that the exploration of our hidden capacities must be conducted responsibly, with due regard for the intricacy of our genetic and cognitive frameworks. It's essential that any methods aimed at unlocking or modifying our inherent potential be approached with careful consideration and under the guidance of accomplished experts or by following robust ethical and scientific principles. Ultimately, the journey is as significant as the destination, and our objective is to facilitate an authentic, measured, and conscientious progression towards unveiling your talents and abilities.

I have found that one's potential is best activated through purpose-driven living. Engaging yourself in a purposeful endeavor often also provides social support and an infrastructure framework that helps to activate the gestation of skills and abilities that are appropriate to your life and work. Just as a fish who has to adapt to new more powerful currents becomes a stronger swimmer, embracing purposes that require your growth may be the most reliable and safest road to evolving the expanded abilities needed to fulfill the role that you and the universe wish you to occupy.

Another Theory of Relativity

Einstein's Theory of Relativity revolutionized our understanding of the universe. It unveiled profound insights into the intertwined nature of time, space, and energy, marking an epochal shift in the realm of physics. Yet, let's explore another theory, one that posits the real potency of "relativity" lies not in atomic forces but in the relationships we nurture.

This concept might seem familiar to those who have experienced the perks of influential friendships or robust familial ties. Consider individuals who invest fortunes to attend elite universities. The true value derived from these institutions often lies not solely in the quality of education but predominantly in the relationships and alliances formed there. Most of these connections exist within one or two degrees of separation, extending our personal and professional networks.

However, the Theory of Relativity I propose pushes beyond these first- and second-degree connections. It explores the power vested in alignments formed through shared purpose and shared consciousness. These connections, unconstrained by physical boundaries or societal distinctions like race, sex, and age, bind us in a profound, universal sense of unity. I have witnessed versions of this dynamic with teens playing online gaming with team mates or opponents that may be plugged into the platform from anywhere in the world.

In our era of artificial intelligence, tools like WayBeyond.ai can amplify the potential of these connections, fostering a synchronicity that propels us to unprecedented levels of collaboration and interaction. These platforms aid the exchange of ideas across geographical and cultural divides, encouraging the creation of a globally unified, like-minded Crew for Spaceship Earth.

Now, I would like to add another dimension to this Theory of Relativity that ventures beyond the physical universe, transcending into the realm of spiritual connections and the power inherent in them. Before proceeding, I will add a personal note that adding this part of my Theory of Relativity to this book is not a decision taken lightly. This is a deeply personal revelation, an aspect of the theory that suggests the true power of "relativity" might not just come from our physical connections but also from our links with spiritual and eternal relatives across the vast expanse of time-space dimensions.

It's essential to understand that what I'm about to share may not be something everyone will consciously experience or be able to fit into their reality model. Nevertheless, I firmly believe it exists and remains active in influencing our collective journey, regardless of what is consciously perceived. Allow me to illustrate this concept with a personal story from the early winter of 1983, which involved the core group of the Dalai Lama and their sacred ceremony they sponsored in New Orleans.

In the early winter of 1983, the Dalai Lama's core group came to New Orleans to anchor one of their most holy temples by establishing a spiritual vortex exactly polar opposite the temple's main altar. The site turned out to align with a vacant lot in an area in New Orleans East where they intended to bury a large number of crystals and artifacts after using them in a ceremony to initiate 100 spiritual adepts from the surrounding area. Their intention is to put them onto the path of Dharma and thereby enable them to help anchor this energy tether. I was fortunate to be one of these people invited to participate in this 3-day ceremony.

The shift from Karma to Dharma, as they explained, involves a transformative change from self-centered actions, causing personal repercussions, "karma," into a collective state of consciousness where the needs of others equals their own. As we align our actions with the needs of the collective living Universe, (what some call God) we become servants of the Divine, guided by intuitive connections with the Creator and the extended family. By acting in favor of the collective's well-being, and carrying out actions for and guided by the

Creator, one transcends individual karma in favor of the group's "dharma," or collective karma.

At the end of the 3rd day, we went one at a time into the center of their circle surrounded by the Dalai Lama's core group. As my turn arose, I stepped into the center of the sacred circle, where I was instructed to ask the ascended masters if they would accept me, turn the wheels of Dharma, and shift my path into alignment. Instantly, my vision went interdimensional. I was now standing on a clear force field in the center of a massive amphitheater where each level contained one thousand arches forming one circular floor, with each arch housing an ascended master sitting on a throne. This assembly spanned across all races, colors, and sizes, with members both human and somewhat different from what I considered human. There were also multiple floors, each with its own 1,000 ascended master. They were stacked one on top of another as far as I could see to a point of infinity and also extended below me as far as I could see; there were many millions of ascended masters in total.

I received their message telepathically because they did not need to vibrate air with vocal cords. They let me know they were all real, although this structure was a construct for my mind to hold them in my limited intellect. They had all once been incarnate beings but had ascended past death's doorways into eternity. They had assembled there for me in that moment through direct conscious extension from wherever and whenever they are in the multiverse, a feat they could do effortlessly at their stage of continuing evolution.

They wanted me to know that I need not be scared or overly concerned about the challenges we faced. The self-serving forces of greed and darkness can never truly join on deep levels of alignment, even with each other, since they serve themselves primarily. While Creator's family are truly aligned on the deepest levels, they can be patient and observe the ongoing drama that occurs in the material planes. There have been more populated worlds throughout the eternal multiverse than there are grains of sand on the earth that have enabled countless souls to incubate and evolve while incarnate bodies.

Therefore, the constructive forces of light and Dharma are never threatened by plots and carrying ons of the selfish lost in greed and darkness any more than we need be concerned if a few hamsters were to squabble over their exercise wheel. Allowing the drama to play out and the participants to learn is part of how Creator grows and matures his primary crop, which is ascended beings. That to be a servant in the Divine Family is a far greater position than to be an emperor controlling an entire material world. I am a servant, I could not want anything more. In reality, I believe there can be nothing more than to be a servant of the Divine.

I want to note that the few participants I spoke to afterward each had very unique and different experiences, because God Consciousness must be translated into forms that we can each receive and understand in our own terms.

Despite what seems to occur through our senses as the sewing needles of bodies, terrestrial, celestial and our own dance in time, while weaving a tapestry of light into the endless carpet of eternity, it is the relatives, which make the real difference. This is Relativity at its best. We are not alone, outnumbered, and outgunned in an immense struggle that is overwhelming and impossible to make a difference. It only appears that way so that we learn to dig deeper, beyond our physical senses and rational minds to hopefully come into awareness with our true reserves of power, our Relativity.

The rest of this topic will be for you to personally consider and assimilate if you so choose to reach out to your extended relatives.

Reintegration of Our Greater Self

In the journey of redefining our place in the world and if so chosen, to transition from a karmic to a dharmic lifestyle, we will encounter profound challenges and transformative opportunities. As we have been rightly reminded, the pivotal change must begin within ourselves; until we shift our perspective and understanding on an individual level, little progress can be made on an external level.

In my younger days, I wrote a school essay that compared capitalism to communism and compared humans to ants, innately communistic beings. Back then, I ardently believed in the pursuit of wealth and power, convinced that communism was incompatible with human nature. Yet, as I reflect on these thoughts, I wonder whether we are inherently self-centered or if the competitive systems we've embraced have shaped us into such individuals. In various cultures, we see the innate willingness to share and support one another, often labeled as "primitive" in contrast to the prevailing norm.

At a pivotal moment, a profound revelation unfolded within me, enlightening my understanding of the higher self. It became clear that true fulfillment lay not in expanding my personal capacities like a wealthy pufferfish, becoming the patriarch of my own clan while inflating my ego to colossal proportions. Instead, I came to embrace the understanding that real abundance is in the art of giving, rather than taking, owning, and consuming less while being a supportive force for collective abundance. As if a veil had lifted, I perceived the interconnectedness of all life, realizing that my growth was intricately linked to the growth of those around me. That we lifted each other and if anything like heaven on earth could ever exist, it would have to exist for everyone. I comprehended that my purpose was to support, uplift, and nurture others, particularly those who are already trying to express good works for the whole.

As this revelation washed over me, I let go of the illusion of separateness and embraced the profound unity that weaves the tapestry of existence. I understood that we are all threads, intricately connected and contributing to the beauty and resilience of the whole fabric. No longer did I see myself as an isolated entity striving for personal gain; instead, I recognized that my path to true self-realization involved supporting the flourishing of others.

In this interconnected symphony of souls, every act of compassion, kindness, and generosity reverberates through the collective consciousness, elevating not just the recipients but also the giver. It is a dance of reciprocity, where the more we give, the more we receive, and the more we receive, the more we can give. Like the boundless ocean tides that constantly exchange energy with the shore, we are part of an endless cycle of sharing and renewal.

Through this shift in perspective, I began finding liberation from many of the narrow confines of my ego-driven desires. I was not as confined to the limiting notion of "I" as a separate entity, but rather, I entered a process of expansion, starting to recognize my emerging role as a co-creator in the grand symphony of life. Each day is an opportunity to embody the essence of service and compassion, recognizing that by uplifting others, I am nurturing the essence and potential of my own being on what may be an infinite journey of growth.

The journey from Karma to Dharma is a transformative one — a journey of shedding the illusion of isolation and embracing our inherent interconnectedness. It is about dissolving the walls that divide us and opening our hearts to the profound truth that we are one, part of a vast cosmic family. Like a dazzling mosaic, we each contribute a unique piece that, when united, forms a masterpiece of unity and diversity.

Despite the hurdles that lie ahead, the realization that we are intimately intertwined with the fate of others becomes our guiding light. We become torchbearers of a new paradigm, where mutual support and collective well-being become the cornerstones of our existence. We recognize that the welfare of one is intertwined with the welfare of all, and that by nurturing the growth of others, we flourish as individuals and as a society.

As we embark on this sacred journey of reintegration, let us remember that the true measure of our greatness lies not in accumulating material wealth or even personal accolades, but in the compassionate footprints we leave on Mother Earth and in the hearts of others. Let us embrace the joy of giving, for it is through giving that we receive the true essence of life. In this dance of interconnectedness, the song of our souls harmonizes with the symphony of existence, and we become the conduits of love and transformation.

This is the calling that resonates in the depths of our being — the call to embrace our greater self and rise together as a global family, hand in hand, heart in heart. It is time to release the shackles of ego-driven pursuits and embrace the path of service and interconnectedness. In doing so, we step into the fullness of our human potential, a potential that can usher in a world where compassion, love, and unity thrive. Together, we can create a symphony of existence that resounds through the ages, a symphony of love and oneness that echoes into eternity.

Activating Our Intuitive Abilities

Have you ever noticed how flies seem to know when we are holding something and cannot shoo them away? Or how your pet seems to read your mind, responding to your thoughts and emotions with an uncanny understanding? These occurrences hint at the innate intuitive nature that pervades the fabric of life. From the buzzing flies to our beloved pets, the body of nature appears to possess a high degree of intuitive capacity, effortlessly sensing and feeling the world around them.

Yet, when it comes to humans, it often seems that we are the least intuitive of all creatures. Our minds are constantly entangled in a web of thoughts and beliefs, obscuring our ability to truly see, sense, or feel the profound truths that surround us. As John Lennon so eloquently expressed in his 1980 song "Beautiful Boy," life happens while we are busy making other plans, suggesting that we are often preoccupied with our mental constructs, missing out on the deeper currents of intuitive wisdom flowing through existence.

In my journey with the Essene order of the Melchizedek Priests, I encountered a profound teaching about Sympathetic Resonance — the harmonization of heart and mind that triggers the pituitary gland to secrete a substance that opens the frontal lobe, enhancing our intuitive capabilities. The Essene order's practices refine the depths of human consciousness, seeking to bridge the gap between the conscious mind and the wisdom of the heart.

The Catholic "sign of the cross," and Trinitarian invocation has deeper roots in the Essene order and carry a profound symbolic meaning. Touching one's right hand to the forehead first (Father — Conscious Mind), then to the lower chest or stomach (Son — Body Mind), then to the left shoulder (Physical Heart), and finally to the right shoulder (Spiritual Heart) before closing both hands together for assent to the forehead (Amen — Frontal Lobe), serves as a powerful reminder to invoke Sympathetic Resonance — the harmonizing of the conscious mind, the body mind, the worldly and spiritual hearts, and the intuitive mind. This Sympathetic Resonance prompts the pituitary gland to secrete a substance that opens the frontal lobe, unlocking greater intuitive capacity in us.

While some may find these concepts a bit outlandish, I am convinced that synchronizing our thoughts with our hearts, bodies, and spirits holds the key to activating our latent intuitive abilities. The act of being open-hearted in our thinking, emotions, and actions would logically and naturally allow us to bypass the defensive mechanisms we have all been taught to adopt in the pursuit of self-preservation in this "Law of The Jungle" physical world.

As we begin to prioritize the needs of others on par or even ahead of our own, we open ourselves to a vast reservoir of intuitive wisdom. By relaxing our defenses and cultivating compassion, empathy, and interconnectedness, we activate our intuitive faculties in a wondrous fashion. It is as if we are reconnecting through mindfulness with the infinite intelligence that flows through all of creation, tapping into the profound harmony of the cosmos.

The scientific evidence on meditation supports the idea that practices like mindfulness open us up to deeper wisdom and intuition. As the studies show, meditation strengthens neural pathways related to attention, emotion regulation, and self-awareness. This allows us to move beyond our usual ego-driven mode of thinking into a more expansive, compassionate awareness.

When we relax our normal defenses and sense of separation from others, we can tap into deeper intuitive faculties, as ancient wisdom traditions have long taught. Modern research is now validating these claims. The strengthened neural foundations developed through meditation allow us to access profound insights and knowledge that typically lie below the surface of our conscious minds.

By cultivating compassion, empathy, and interconnectedness through mindfulness practices, we rewire our brains in ways that activate our capacity for intuition. It's as if we are tapping back into the collective wisdom and intelligence that permeates all of life. The research shows we can enhance our intuitive abilities through consciously developing qualities like presence, equanimity, and open-heartedness.

Here are some key scientific studies on the benefits of meditation and mindfulness:

- A 2011 study by researchers at Harvard found that mindfulness meditation strengthens neural pathways and brain regions associated with attention and emotion regulation. Regular meditators showed increased gray matter density in areas like the prefrontal cortex and hippocampus.
- A 2012 study by Johns Hopkins researchers found that even short-term mindfulness meditation training helped reduce mind wandering and improved focus during tasks. Participants completed just 11 hours of meditation over one month.
- A 2020 meta-analysis published in JAMA Internal Medicine looked at 209 studies on mindfulness-based interventions. It

found mindfulness effectively reduces anxiety, depression, and psychological distress while improving quality of life.

- Researchers at the University of Wisconsin-Madison found in 2022 that mindfulness meditation lowers levels of the stress hormone cortisol. The more years of meditation experience, the greater the cortisol reduction.

- A study in Psychoneuroendocrinology in 2017 found evidence that mindfulness meditation positively impacts regions of the brain related to attention, emotion regulation, and self-awareness.

The growing body of research continues to demonstrate the cognitive, psychological, and physiological benefits of regular meditation and mindfulness practices. The studies show it can lead to structural and functional changes in key brain regions that support focus, resilience, and well-being.

Here are some examples of prominent innovators and creators who successfully leveraged intuition and inner wisdom:

- Steve Jobs frequently discussed how intuition and creativity were central to his work at Apple and Pixar. He practiced meditation and credited it with allowing him to tap into deeper inner guidance. Jobs attributed key innovations like the GUI interface and iPad design to intuitive breakthroughs.

- Albert Einstein said his scientific discoveries came from intuition and inspiration, not just rational thinking. He believed developing intuition allowed him to conceive radical new ideas like the general theory of relativity. Einstein recommended cultivating intuition through activities like music and imagination.

- Nikola Tesla was renowned for his powerful imagination and ability to visualize detailed inventions intuitively. He said his innovative designs for motors and electrical systems came directly from his "mind's eye" through visualization rather than logical analysis.

- The acclaimed filmmaker Ingmar Bergman wrote of how he would often intuit entire scenes and details of his films without consciously thinking them through. He believed tapping into his subconscious imagination was central to his cinematic creativity.

- Marie Curie attributed her discovery of radium and pioneering work in radioactivity to an inner intuitive sense that guided her research. She cultivated this ability through activities like playing the piano, which she said stimulated inspiration.

- Rick Rubin, the legendary record executive and producer, in his inspired book, The Creative Act: A Way of Being, discusses how major recording artists rely heavily upon inspiration as their source. Rick hired our small production crew to make several music videos for his artist in the 90s, and I know firsthand that he is a visionary and a serious business person. He always expected us to deliver the goods on even low budgets.

These examples demonstrate how cultivating intuition and inner wisdom has been central to human creativity and innovation across fields. Unlocking our deeper faculties can lead to transformative breakthroughs.

Both modern science and ancient wisdom traditions concur that there are levels of interconnectedness and intelligence within us that go far beyond our typical conscious awareness. By developing our intuitive faculties, we can align with these deeper currents.

Modern research at the frontiers of neuroscience, physics, and consciousness studies confirms that our minds extend far beyond our physical brains. Quantum physics reveals entanglement and instantaneous interconnectivity permeate the cosmos. Studies show our brains exhibit quantum effects, suggesting consciousness itself is quantum in nature. This implies deeper levels of collective intelligence and intuition we can tap into.

Similarly, ancient wisdom from traditions like Buddhism, Taoism, shamanism, and mysticism universally point to these deeper realities existing within and around us. Practices like meditation, vision quests, and shamanic journeys were developed to quiet the thinking mind and allow intuitive ways of knowing to arise. Indigenous cultures understand intuition as the ability to tap into the "spirit wisdom" that permeates all creation.

This ancient worldview aligns with leading-edge science. So when we develop our intuition through mindfulness, expansion of awareness, and holistic practices, we unveil our connections to universal fields of intelligence. We transcend our isolated egos to perceive how we are all expressions of one interdependent cosmic web. Great intuition comes from living and creating in accord with the fundamental unity and wisdom that grounds all things.

My hope and belief is that as we embrace a path of intuitive awakening, meditation, and mindfulness, we will naturally emerge as the crew of Spaceship Earth, ready to handle the challenges of the day with expanded capabilities. Like seasoned sailors navigating the turbulent seas, our intuition will serve as a compass, guiding us through the unknown waters with confidence and grace.

The journey into the realm of intuition is not one that can be simply intellectualized or understood through words alone. It is a journey of experiential discovery, one that each of us must undertake for ourselves. As you open your heart and mind to the possibilities of intuitive activation, you will witness subtle shifts in your perceptions and interactions with the world.

Try it for yourself — embrace the harmony of heart and mind, prioritize the needs of others, and let your intuition be your guiding star. Only through personal experience can you fully grasp the profundity of this transformation. As you embark on this journey of intuitive exploration, you may find yourself awakening to a higher truth, one that transcends the limitations of the mind and expands your awareness to encompass the vast interconnectedness of all life.

So, take a step into the realm of intuitive knowing — where the wisdom of the heart and the clarity of the mind dance in perfect harmony. Embrace the innate intuitive nature that resides within you, and let it guide you on an extraordinary adventure of self-discovery and connection with the greater tapestry of existence. Your intuitive capacity is waiting to be awakened; it is time to heed the call and embark on this marvelous journey of reconnection with the essence of who you truly are. Only by trying this for yourself can you find the truth in this teaching from the ancient past.

What Do We Need to Shift?

Amidst the hurdles, we must embark on a profound shift in our perception of reality, acknowledging that:

- The needs of others are as vital as our own — for in caring for them, we care for ourselves.
- Supporting others' paths of growth and empowering their highest expressions of value enriches our own lives.
- True success is measured by what we contribute, not what we take.
- Our physical well-being is intricately tied to the health of the planetary biosphere.
- Our emotional well-being thrives when the collective's well-being is nurtured.
- The still-living genetic codes of all life are our most valuable asset.
- Preserving energy resources for future generations is a sacred duty we must uphold.

- Minimizing our footprint of damage, and even transforming it into a positive force, is a noble aspiration.

As we redefine success and realign our focus, we begin to build a future where mutual support and care become the pillars of our existence. This transformation is not a mere utopian concept; it is an imperative axiom that every individual must embrace. It is a pathway to authentic evolution, joy, and a profound enhancement of our self-image and sense of value.

Imagine a world where we each contribute our unique gifts to uplift one another, nurturing an interconnected ecosystem of thriving souls. Just as a symphony's harmonious melodies arise from each instrument playing in concert, we can create a symphony of human potential, resonating with the rhythms of life itself. Imagine where this world will be in 100 years, in 1,000 years, in 1,000,000 years. Life without end, personal growth with no limits.

Uplifting Every Member

Consider how, when we water a parched plant, it blossoms and contributes to the beauty of the garden. Similarly, when we invest in the growth and empowerment of others, we cultivate a society where each individual's brilliance flourishes. I cannot help but notice how in America, we do not always see the rehabilitation of "broken" people as a viable solution. Instead, we as a society tend to cast them aside or plow them into the ground, as if they were irredeemable. However, there are more civilized countries right now here on earth that understand the potential of rehabilitation. They recognize that nurturing and supporting individuals in their journey of healing is far less costly, both morally and economically, than resorting to incarceration or disregarding their needs and humanity.

In these more enlightened societies, the concept of rehabilitation becomes a cornerstone of their justice systems. They understand that behind every shattered life lies the potential for transformation and growth. Just as a gardener tends to a struggling plant with care, providing it with the right environment, nourishment, and support to flourish, these countries offer their citizens a chance at redemption and restoration.

By embracing the value of rehabilitation, these societies give individuals the tools and resources they need to rebuild their lives and become contributing members of the community once more. They view the act of healing as a collective responsibility, recognizing that when one person is lifted up, the entire community benefits. This interdependent network of support elevates us all, enabling us to co-create a shared reality of abundance and fulfillment.

It is a profound shift in perspective, akin to seeing a garden not just as a collection of individual plants but as a living ecosystem where each component thrives in harmony with the others. Just as a thriving garden supports a diverse array of plant life, so too does a society that prioritizes rehabilitation foster the growth and diversity of its people.

In contrast, societies that forsake rehabilitation often perpetuate a cycle of suffering. By discarding those who have stumbled or strayed, they deny the potential for redemption and hinder the growth of the collective. Such an approach mirrors a garden where withered plants are discarded without regard for the potential they once held or the contribution they could have made to the garden's beauty.

As we contemplate the importance of rehabilitation, let us remember that every life has inherent value and the capacity for transformation. Just as a compassionate gardener tends to each plant with love and patience, we must approach our fellow human beings with the same compassion and understanding.

By investing in rehabilitation and providing opportunities for growth, we sow the seeds of hope and renewal. We create a society where individuals are not condemned to a lifetime of hardship but are empowered to rise above their past and blossom into their fullest potential.

Ultimately, embracing the concept of rehabilitation is not only a humane and just approach; it is also a pragmatic one. When we believe in the power of redemption and invest in the growth of all individuals, we build a society that thrives on the strength of its collective diversity. Just as a flourishing garden is a testament to the gardener's care, a flourishing society is a testament to its commitment to supporting and uplifting every member.

Uplifting Ourselves

This transformation requires a personal calling to action — a resolute commitment to making the necessary shifts within ourselves. Let us envision each action we take as a ripple that emanates far beyond our immediate sphere, creating a wave of positive change that reverberates through the collective consciousness. A lovely friend in New Orleans, Roger, whom we lost early to AIDs, elucidated how every gesture and action we take is part of a dance, a grand ballet appreciated by the Angels. I loved his view and some of us tried to move more gracefully forward in life due to his influence.

Picture the concept of "self" extending beyond the boundaries of our physical bodies to encompass all life forms, connecting us, cells within a vast organism of existence. Just as a single cell within our bodies serves the greater organism, we, too, are indispensable fibers in the cosmic fabric.

Let us remember that the very air we breathe is shared by billions, transcending borders and ideologies. When we care for the air, water, and earth, we care for the well-being of countless beings. Each act of ecological stewardship becomes an offering of love and gratitude to the planet that sustains us.

As we traverse this path of reintegration, we are akin to gardeners tending to the flourishing garden of humanity. Our individual contributions may seem modest, but collectively, they cultivate a world of abundance, harmony, and interconnectedness.

We are not isolated islands in the vast ocean of existence; we are waves of consciousness, intermingling and shaping the trajectory of humanity's evolution. With each mindful decision and compassionate gesture, we unleash the potential for an extraordinary future — one where selflessness, unity, and co-creation flourish.

In conclusion, let us embrace this transformative journey, nurturing our greater self and recognizing that we are both architects and beneficiaries of a world founded on love, service, and collective well-being. Together, let us weave a symphony of existence, a grand ballet, each note and move harmonizing with the greater cosmic melody. This is the key to our true evolution, our joy, and our innate sense of value. This is our sacred calling — to reclaim our place as stewards of the planet and champions of one another's dreams. It is time to reintegrate our greater self, to embark on a journey of profound interconnectedness, and to co-create a future that reflects the highest expressions of our shared humanity.

XI.
AWAKENING INTO OUR COLLECTIVE DESTINY

As we conclude this phase of our journey together, I'm reminded of the immortal words of Khalil Gibran, who said, "Your pain is the breaking of the shell that encloses your understanding." While the challenges we face today may seem daunting, and the task Herculean, to transform the Mad Race to Nowhere into a pilgrimage where we Gracefully manifest the true calling in our hearts and Illumined minds to transform our role into Caregivers who responsibly manage Earth. I ask you to Re-Call that your deeper purpose is to mindfully advance up the octaves of our own version of Jacob's Ladder into the Heavenly Realms of your own divine expression.

If Earth is our spaceship, and we are its crew, then our first responsibility is to ensure the ship remains functional, sustainable, and harmonious. Let us reiterate the key specific steps towards Activating The Crew of Spaceship Earth that aid us in our Pivotal Planetary Transformation:

Realigning with Nature

- Align with Nature's Wisdom: Adopt sustainable, regenerative practices informed by Indigenous cultures and cyclical systems. Partner with nature, not dominate it.
- Enshrine Rights for Nature: Grant natural entities like rivers and forests legal rights. Respect nature's intrinsic value, apart from human utility.

Restructuring Systems and Measures

- Redefine Progress: Evolve beyond GDP and material consumption as measures of success. Define progress by well-being, sustainability and equitable distribution of resources.
- Cultivate Systems Thinking: Understand the interdependence of individuals, societies, and nature. Make choices considering impacts on the wider system.

Transforming Mindsets and Values

- Shift from Consumer to Contributor Mindset: Recognize our role as stewards of Spaceship Earth, not exploiters. Move from an extractive to a nurturing approach.
- Prioritize Innovation for Good: Leverage technology and creativity to solve pressing challenges like climate change, not deepen consumerism. Focus innovation on society's needs.
- Champion Diversity and Inclusion: Ensure all groups are represented in decision-making and wealth distribution. Value diversity while promoting unity.

Building Community and Relationships

- Foster Collective Awakening: Enable grassroots movements and amplify marginalized voices to spark systemic change. Transform through community.
- Rehabilitate our Relationships: Heal rifts between groups, classes, races, generations, and nations. Rebuild our social fabric and collective potential.

Nurturing Human Potential

- Promote Holistic Education: Develop curricula that impart social, emotional, ecological, and spiritual intelligence alongside technical skills. Take a lifewide approach to learning.
- Commit to Continuous Refinement: Keep evolving by soliciting feedback, hearing what criticism arises, and challenging outdated norms. No single solution is final.

Envisioning a Healthy Earth for the Future

True visionaries don't merely plan for the next decade; they envision millennia. A world where our ecosystems aren't just surviving but thriving, where the harmony between man and nature is a given, not an exception. This vision should not remain confined to philosophical discussions but needs to be translated into actionable goals.

Engaging communities in these visions can birth tangible blueprints. Localized, ground-up solutions can be woven into the digital realm, with platforms like WayBeyond.ai, translating them into synergistic models that can be scaled up, replicated, and refined. This iterative process, grounded in community wisdom and augmented by digital prowess, can guide us towards that envisioned Earth.

Envisioning a Healthy Earth for the Future

True visionaries don't merely plan for the next decade; they envision millennia. A world where our ecosystems aren't just surviving but thriving, where the harmony between man and nature is a given, not an exception. This vision should not remain confined to philosophical discussions but needs to be translated into actionable goals.

True visionaries think not in terms of years but eons, envisioning futures unconstrained by current limitations. We can reimagine an Earth where ecosystems flourish in vibrant harmony, from lush rainforests to vibrant coral reefs. Where humans are truly humane to each other and the land around them is nurtured as a living being, the other creatures, are respected as sovereign members, not consumer commodities. This vision will not remain abstract but will be translated into concrete goals. What steps will restore forests, rivers, and topsoil? How can we transition industries to sustainability? What policies will promote regeneration? Dreamers, artists, manifestors, and scientists will collaborate in new ways producing solutions previously unimagined.

Local communities worldwide will share solutions tailored to their lands that reinforce their unique culture. Digital tools like WayBeyond.ai will help integrate this knowledge, while simulations assess and composite potential outcomes, and prototype and refine models, from ecovillages to green transit, that uplift all life.

Drawing from nature's resilience, we will create balance as an extension of our centered being. We will learn the language in nature's blueprint, from the biomimicry in Earth's wisdom, from termite mounds to hummingbirds' seemingly impossible flight, from the bats' sonic navigation to the exoskeletal brilliance of insects, we will express technological innovation from regenerative food production, to fuel and pollution free energy, agroforestry will integrate trees into farmlands, enriching soil, urban architecture will include rooftop gardens and ample greenspaces.

As we rediscover ancestral knowledge and live in cyclical modern villages, progressive youth will lead movements for change while Indigenous elders share stewardship wisdom. With empathy and diligence, we will convince those still invested in exploitation to transform businesses and policies into ways of renewal.

While the road ahead will still hold many twists and turns, our expanding consciousness will illuminate the path and our hearts will integrate our decisions. As we quiet internal turbulence, insights will reveal how thread by thread, strand by strand, we will weave our vision into our reality. This is the growth that we want and therefore it is what will be.

As alliances between activists, social entrepreneurs, and enlightened policymakers form and blossom, systems will change rapidly, as old paradigms fade amid new social ideals. Just as shorelines transform gradually until the moment the rising tide surges in, our incremental progress will gain momentum.

The key is balancing pragmatism with transcendent visions — navigating today's realities while expanding mental horizons. As we consciously evolve, elevating ethics and enlightened use of technology, we will steer our planet towards an abundant future.

This is now our shared duty — to translate the dream of an idyllic Earth into bite-sized goals and cooperative action. With nature as a mentor, diversity as a strength, and technology as an ally, we can transform this fragile biosphere into a thriving "Garden of Eden" where all species harmoniously abide.

Embracing Our Proclivity to Evolve

Human evolution encompasses more than physiological adaptations; it's a dance of consciousness, intellect, spirit, and collective sharing. Recognize that our presence in this era is not random, it is no accident. We are endowed with the intellectual and emotional tools, and communal tools to navigate the challenges before us and innovate solutions to meet those challenges.

These trials we face together are part of an intricate curriculum in our planetary 'Omni-University', to hone our capabilities, pushing the boundaries of what we know, understand, and can achieve. Our codes carry genetic memories of our past, Indigenous wisdom passed down through time immemorial that grounds us into our deep roots with the land. Stories from prophets and mystics reveal the cycles of destruction and renewal, a testament to our inherent capacity to adapt, grow, and flourish. Visionaries throughout history dared to reimagine civilization, assuring us that we can also do what we need to now.

When we connect with the true pulse of life, we discover her innate artistry, our minds expand, and our desires refocus beyond selfish greed to embrace the collective needs. We shed old shells of separation and ignorance, transforming into agents of compassion. Modern science shows our intricate biochemical wiring, with neurons and DNA encoding intelligence far beyond what is manifested. While our technology has outpaced ethical maturity, birthing weapons that could annihilate yet also tools that uplift, we come from a lineage that laid the foundation of many Universes. Through challenge, our capabilities are magnified. With empathy and contemplation, we form a collective heart and conscience to better guide us in symphony and choir writing a new song of humanity's key choices and narrative.

We are not passive participants in some predetermined plan but co-creators of our unfolding destiny. Today we hold the pen, inked with hard-won knowledge, visions of futures near and far, and an awakening to life's sanctity. With intention, we etch our legacy upon new pages.

Though the task is monumental, our genetic codes have long prepared for this hour. They whisper what greatness lies not beyond us but incubates within, awaiting our activation, and spiritual unfolding. We are the children of stardust and sunlight, crafted by eons of flickering stars and blooming biospheres, culminating in our minds that ponder and pen life's deepest mysteries. This is our birthright hour, our calling, our duty — to tend the living earth so her abundance nurtures us and all creatures great and small. With each humane act of compassion, we excavate our potential, we mend our broken hearts, we generate cycles of healing and fulfillment, we author a future with wisdom, and we guide Spaceship Earth into our destiny among the stars.

The Stars Start Here

The vastness of space invites us to ponder and explore: could we really be the sole bearers of consciousness in this vast expanse? Some might ask that question, others already know the answer. We are not. If other civilizations, advanced in wisdom and technology, are watching our progress, are they waiting for a sign that we have matured as a species? Almost certainly. What would it mean to be accepted into a galactic society? As we step up as the Crew of Spaceship Earth with alacrity and dedication, we may just find out that answer.

The idea, whether reality or fantasy to some, serves as an invaluable mirror, reflecting our current state and where we ought to be. If we aspire to be part of a galactic community, we must first pass our probationary inspection and prove our mettle by harmonizing our home, our Spaceship Earth. This isn't merely about technological advancements but, more crucially, about spiritual, communal, and ecological maturity. Space is not a way for us to escape our destruction of Earth. That will not happen. It is our path to share the lessons we are about to master and demonstrate to the ascended masters of the Metaverse our skill as planetary caregivers.

While the stars might seem distant, they serve as a poignant reminder of our potential, our potential nest playground after we graduate. The steps we take today, the communities we nurture, the visions we craft, and the challenges we overcome, all pave the path towards our stellar destiny. And so, as custodians of Earth and potential ambassadors of humanity to the cosmos, the call to action is clear: let's awaken, evolve, and shine.

As the sun rises, casting away the obscurity of the night, so can the collective consciousness of humanity, inch towards a brighter, more harmonious destiny. Drawing from the vast reservoir of ideas and philosophies explored in previous sections, we understand that our collective destiny is an intricate dance of awakening, an alignment into our true Dharma that we share as sentient beings becoming more divine. Let us reshape our world to honor purpose over profit. Like healthy cells fulfilling our roles, let us support each person so they can contribute their full talents towards our collective thriving; let us respect and nurture our Mother Earth so she can in turn increase her bounty onto our banquet of cornucopia. Let us embrace all forms of life on Earth being their own unique divine expressions within the intricate lattice of life. Let us keep our feet on the rich soil and grasses we have nurtured, rather than the hot pavement that we once called progress. Let us respect the gem of Creator in any of the myriad names, perspectives, and directions that the people of the Earth may use to refer to the Great One. We share this path together. We are One.

XII.
ANTICIPATING QUESTIONS AND OBJECTIONS

In a work covering such a wide array of unconventional ideas, there are bound to be questions, counter-perspectives, and critiques that arise. I welcome such diverse discourse, as the path forward necessitates holding space for a plurality of thought and continual questioning of assumed norms.

In this spirit of open inquiry, I have tried to anticipate some areas of contention or confusion. I offer responses not as immutable answers, but rather as an initial contribution to ongoing dialogue. My hope is these questions provide launching pads to collective exploration of the nuances embedded within this work.

Question: You speak often of a "collective awakening" but isn't meaningful change driven by individual actions?

Response: You raise a fair point. While collective shift is emphasized, individual consciousness, initiative, and responsibility are the seeds of larger transformation. It is said that if the leading 5% of the population embraces a change the others will follow. The change must be rooted individually in our personal values and behavior patterns before it will fully bloom in our society.

Question: If we move towards more localized economies, won't that encourage insularity and impede global cooperation?

Response: Localization needs to balance with global collaboration, which has inherent advantages from large scale. Fostering resilient communities shouldn't compromise our ability to exchange ideas, resources, and culture globally. Artisan, locally produced products tend to be more pricey so the patrons must appreciate the value to pay more. With care, the two can complement each other.

Question: How can we enact such sweeping changes when people are so divided on politics, economics, and social issues?

Response: Many divisions are founded in excess competition, described as Wetiko by some Native Americans. Our divisions shouldn't deter us but rather inspire us to find common ground. By identifying shared hopes and values, we can nurture understanding and purpose. Change emerges gradually through changing hearts and perspectives.

Question: Many argue we need a radical systemic overhaul, not gradual reforms. Why focus on incremental change?

Response: It's a valid stance that structural change is needed. However, lasting change often happens steadily as mindsets evolve. Well-intentioned radicalism can also yield unintended disruptions and system breakdowns in the process that would be excessively painful for society. A balanced approach may be integrating the two.

Question: Many of the examples and models seem derived from Western thought. How might these proposals apply to non-Western cultures?

Response: As the author, I value many other cultures and models. The ideas here need to be adapted contextually, integrating non-Western worldviews. Cross-cultural dialogue to bridge Eastern, Indigenous, and other modes of thought is vital and one of the goals of creating WayBeyond.ai as a worldwide interface.

Question: Practices like biomass reuse seem unrealistic to implement in complex modern cities and industries. Are these truly scalable?

Response: I admit real solutions face adoption obstacles, but we must expand our notion of what's possible. Human biomass reuse is now in practice, but needs to be refined to be truly beneficial on a mass scale. With innovation and political will, ideas like biomass reuse can gain feasibility, but we need thoughtful transition plans.

Question: While appealing, idealistic visions of the future rarely match reality. Aren't you setting unrealistic expectations?

Response: This is a fair critique. While inspired by idealism, the intention is to spark imaginative thinking and expand our sense of potential. Without clear direction, change is far more difficult. The pragmatics of implementing our shared direction will require nuance consideration that will only be addressed fully by the Crew of Spaceship Earth.

Question: Is "Spaceship Earth" just a metaphor, or are you suggesting Earth is actually a vessel traveling through space?

- Response: "Spaceship Earth" is primarily a metaphor first introduced by visionaries like Buckminster Fuller. It underscores the idea that Earth, as a biologic or planetary vessel, has limited resources and that its inhabitants are collectively responsible for its care as it journeys through the cosmos.

Objection: Traditional Indigenous practices might not scale to address global challenges.

- Response: While it's true that Indigenous practices are tailored to the nuances of the local environments, the underlying philosophies of harmony with nature and sustainable living can provide guiding principles to shape large-scale initiatives.

Question: How can we balance technological advancements with returning to older, Indigenous ways of life?

- Response: This is more of a joyful undertaking than a problem. As we balance the best of both models: using technology to facilitate sustainable practices while adopting the philosophical tenets of Indigenous wisdom we will rediscover and value our harmony with nature.

Objection: The concept of "M Space" and "Creator" seems religious. Is this book promoting a particular belief system?
- o Response: This book doesn't advocate for a specific religion. The terms "M Space" and "Creator" are used to capture a universal essence recognized by quantum physics, various philosophies and beliefs. It is intended to be inclusive and welcoming of all interpretations.

Question: How practical is it to rehabilitate degraded areas, especially in urban centers?
- o Response: It is very practical and beneficial to rehabilitate degraded areas, although it is a multi-faceted process. In urban centers, this could mean creating green spaces, vertical gardens, or urban farming. The key is adaptive strategies that consider the value of preserving nature habitats, establishing renewed urban areas with goals that consider local conditions and resources.

Objection: You mention "Fractal Patterns" and the Hermetic axiom. Isn't this a bit esoteric for a book on pragmatic solutions?
- o Response: While it may seem esoteric, by our nature, we are spiritual beings inhabiting physical bodies. Recognizing recurring patterns in nature and society can offer profound insights into problem-solving and strategy formulation. By understanding these patterns, we can approach challenges holistically.

Question: What do you mean by human biomass redistribution?

- Response: Earth to earth, dust to dust. As humans dominate Earth's biomass, it's essential to recognize the impact we have. Non-toxic human biomass redistribution refers to the idea of ensuring our impact, even in terms of waste, is channeled back into nature sustainably, aiding in soil creation and combating desertification.

Objection: Isn't the reliance on a divine or spiritual reality too subjective to base practical solutions upon?

- Response: We do not need to rely upon divine or spiritual reality to be influenced by recognizing its inherent wisdom. The reference to a broader universal order serves as a philosophical foundation, yet practical solutions and intuitive insights can resonate with readers irrespective of their spiritual beliefs.

Question: You critique excessive wealth accumulation but seem to promote your own initiatives and models quite a bit. Isn't that contradictory?

Response: This is a fair critique. I intend the ARC model, WayBeyond platform, and other initiatives to be freely accessible resources, not proprietary assets. They are envisioned as community-owned utilities and assets designed to increase the abundance and sustainability of our species, not make myself or our core group monetarily wealthy. I will endeavor to be mindful of collective advancement rather than self-promotion.

Question: There are many references to spiritual concepts like "God" and "divine essence" without much supporting evidence. Why should rational readers take these seriously?

Response: I concede that some of the spiritual perspectives shared in this work may seem unsupported from a rational lens attached to a materialistically oriented brain. My intention is to expand material perception and enrich the discourse with a diversity of worldviews to consider based on their individual inclinations.

Question: How are we to fund massive public programs and system reforms with the national debt already so high? Won't these proposals be infeasible?

Response: You raise a pragmatic concern, particularly for the wealthy who do not want their accumulated currency to be diluted. However, when an investment in people and planet return increased ecological and social health, this is a real return, not just paper wealth. I believe humanity's deep resilience and collective ingenuity can find ways to align vision and practicality.

Question: There is a lot of criticism of capitalism but little mention of the tremendous progress it has facilitated. Aren't you overlooking the upsides?

Response: I have attempted to describe some of capitalism's benefits, and credit for its role in driving innovation and prosperity. My critiques target unrestrained "crony capitalism" and living lavishly off of passive wealth. Implemented conscientiously, capitalism can be recalibrated to align with societal and ecological priorities. The aim is balance, not wholesale abolition.

I welcome additional perspectives, as the questions raised in this book deserve ongoing reflection and debate. It is through such pluralistic participation that the solutions for our collective future will emerge, synthesized from our shared wisdom.

Glossary of Terms

Awakening: A transformative realization or coming to consciousness. In the context of the book, it implies a collective understanding of our role as caregivers of Spaceship Earth.

Biomass Redistribution: Refers to the strategy of balancing the impact humans have on Earth, particularly in redistributing organic waste in ways that benefit the environment, such as soil creation.

Creator: A term used in the book to denote a divine or universal force, source, or consciousness. It's a neutral term that intends to resonate across different belief systems.

Dualism: The juxtaposition of two opposing factors or concepts, often hinting at complementary characteristics that can offer deeper insights when combined.

Fractal Patterns: Recurring structures, sequences, or motifs observed across different scales in the universe, from the microscopic to the cosmic.

Indigenous Wisdom: The collective knowledge and practices of Indigenous cultures, rooted in sustainability, community, and harmony with nature.

Joyful Alchemists: A creative collective focused on transformation and positive change, drawing inspiration from both the mystical and pragmatic realms.

M Space: Represents the omnipresence of the "Creator" or universal consciousness. This term captures the inherent yet often unseen force active within our surroundings and minds.

Spaceship Earth: A metaphor popularized by thinkers like Buckminster Fuller, describing Earth as a vessel with limited resources, emphasizing the shared responsibility of its inhabitants.

Sustainability: A principle of using resources in a way that meets current needs without compromising the ability of future generations to meet theirs.

Equity: In a social context, it's about fairness, ensuring everyone has access to the same opportunities, and adjusting shares based on individual needs or abilities.

Compassion: A deep awareness of the suffering of another, coupled with the wish to relieve it.

Gnosis: Spiritual knowledge derived from personal experience rather than traditional teachings, scriptures, or external world perceptions.

Paradox: A statement or situation that might seem contradictory or opposed to common sense, but upon closer inspection, might reveal an underlying truth.

Quantum Physics: A branch of physics studying the tiniest particles and waves, often revealing phenomena that challenge our everyday understanding of reality.

Made in the USA
Columbia, SC
29 October 2024